# THE PROPHETIC WORD TO THE NATIONS

A Compilation of Prophetic Utterances From 2017 – 2022

Apostle Dr. Steve Lyston

The Prophetic Word To The Nations
A Compilation of Prophetic Utterances from 2017 - 2022

Copyright © 2022 Apostle Steve Lyston
Library of Congress Control Number: 2022952101
ISBN: 978-1-7359220-3-4
All rights reserved. No part of this publication may be reproduced, or transmitted in any form or by any means, electronic or mechanical including photocopying, recording, or by any information storage and retrieval system, without prior permission in writing from the copyright owner.
Edited by: Marsha A. McCormack and Michelle R. Lyston
Cover Design by: Johann D. A. Williams
Scripture quotations marked "NKJV" are taken from The New King James Version / Thomas Nelson Publishers, Nashville: Thomas Nelson Publishers. Copyright © 1982. Used by permission. All rights reserved.

This book was printed in Columbia, South Carolina in the United States of America

# DEDICATION

This book is dedicated to the Triune God – God the Father, Jesus the Son and the Holy Spirit of God.

It is also dedicated to every true believer in Christ Jesus who desires a deeper walk in the prophetic.

It is also dedicated to RWOMI Christian University and RWOMI School of the Prophets.

# THANK YOUs

I thank the Triune God our Father, Jesus Christ His Son and the Holy Spirit for His Divine Guidance, Protection and for allowing us the privilege and honor of receiving and releasing His prophetic utterances.

Thank you also to:

Bishop Dr. Doris Hutchinson
Pastor Dr. Michelle Lyston
Pastor Nadra Brotherton
Prophetess Pastor Sophia DiMuccio
Pastor O. Onesto Jolly

# TABLE OF CONTENTS

|  |  | Page |
|---|---|---|
| Dedication |  |  |
| Thank Yous |  |  |
| Introduction |  | 6 |
| Chapter 1 | 2017 | 7 |
| Chapter 2 | 2018 | 26 |
| Chapter 3 | 2019 | 112 |
| Chapter 4 | 2020 | 179 |
| Chapter 5 | 2021 | 214 |
| Chapter 6 | 2022 | 238 |
| Bibliography |  | 324 |

# INTRODUCTION

Amos 3: 7 says, *"Surely the Lord God does nothing, Unless He reveals His secret to His servants the prophets."*

It is critical for us all to know that God speaks and is always speaking. If man would only heed His voice – obey His voice, the price we are paying now globally through the pandemic, climate change and so on, we would not be paying.

Why is there such a great desire for people to seek direction for psychics, soothsayers, shamans, and so on, while we ignore the true, authentic voice of the Lord through His servants. A great section of the Church has also fallen into the trap of ignoring the prophetic word of the Lord.

In this second compilation of prophetic utterances from the Lord spanning 2017 to 2022, you will see what the Lord has said and what has come to pass, what will come to pass and can be a guide for people and nations to engage in wise planning especially in the areas of farming/agriculture, environmental issues and security-related issues – individually or nationally. It is a book that will benefit generations to come.

Never belittle or demean the prophetic utterances of God our Creator, because the prophetic word is vital for all aspects of our existence.

# 2017

# THE PROPHETIC WORD OF THE LORD
Received May 3, 2017

Single ladies, please shun the very appearance of evil in this season. Do not be enticed in this season – especially but not only to go to the beach. There is a man that will be ministered to. He will be very handsome, but he has the spirit lust. Do not be in any long conversations with this person just minister to him and go.

All the single people must keep themselves circumspect and walk upright in His sight. Because you are about to cross a threshold.

What the Lord will show you about the different heads of nations and you will be seeing it on a billboard. The full body picture and bullet points beside the person.

There are going to be problems in Andrew Holness' marriage. The Lord will be speaking to his wife, and she is not going to put up with certain things.

There are 6 member states in the GA that are going to be against each other because of strong disagreements on certain issues. France, Sweden, Kenya, USA, China, Russia. The Secretary General will try to keep things peaceable. These countries are going to be spying on each other.

# THE PROPHETIC WORD OF THE LORD
## Received August 5, 2017

*Through Apostle Dr. Steve Lyston and Bishop Dr. Doris Hutchinson*

The Lord says, "Another Step" He is calling the Body of Christ to take another step of Faith, another step of Holiness, another step of readiness because the rapture can be anytime. Another step of Soul-winning.

John 10 – this is the season of exposure. The true shepherds versus wolves and hirelings and false sheep. In the same way that we have false sheep. True sheep know the true shepherd's voice. False sheep follow false shepherds. If they were true, they would have a desire for the Word. True sheep stay in God's presence and study His word and will not be easily deceived. There is great deception coming. The true heart will know His voice while the false hear will follow others. We will see the rise of the Pharisees because they were not true sheep.

Jesus wants His people to know that He is the Good Shepherd and there is only one Door and one Way and it is He is that Door. Many will come and say there are other ways of salvation, but Jesus is the only Savior. When we go in He gives us safety and in our going out He gives green pastures. Jesus is the Good Shepherd who died for the sheep and carrying the cross daily is key to Christianity. True sheep do not follow false shepherds. Satan is a thief – and he came to kill steal and destroy. He presents a false way of life.

***Hirelings*** are those who engaged solely in self-preservation. They pose as shepherds but are not. The purpose of hirelings is to fleece the sheep – not to protect them. Hirelings don't protect the sheep from the wolves, neither do they care for the sheep. The Lord said false prophets, false apostles or false shepherds have no concern for the sheep. There main concern is their money, their fame, and maintain their position in the marketplace and other places of influence. Most of them are afraid to lose their position and their possessions! (Watch out for those who focus on themselves more than they focus on Christ.)

That is why God is calling His people to a place of intimacy with Him, so that He can speak to His people as there is serious deception ahead.

The Lord says take note of Psalm 33: 10 - 12 which says "The Lord brings the counsel of the nations to nothing; He makes the plans of the peoples of no effect. The counsel of the Lord stands forever, the plans of His heart to all generations. Blessed is the nation whose God is the Lord, the people He has chosen as His own inheritance" Note also Proverbs 19: 21 which reminds us, "There are many plans in a man's heart, nevertheless the Lord's counsel—that will stand."

I believe that these words will be the prophetic word for the remainder of the year. Regardless of the plan individuals, nation leaders, the medical, economic and legal fraternities and those in sports may have - even those planning evil; at the end of the day, only what God's plan is will come to pass. Let us do good and ensure that our plans are in line with God's plans for us. (A great deal of exposure is coming)

# THE PROPHETIC WORD OF THE LORD
**Bishop Dr. Doris Hutchinson**
**August 6, 2017**

For the Lord said, "A lot of evil will be exposed by the end of this year and into the next year. This is a warning as God is not pleased. He has given many warnings and many have not heeded. As exposure takes place, things will become worse. Therefore, all Christians need to live holy lives and all unsaved persons need to repent and turn their lives to Him now. For the Lord says as He exposes the evil and the evil plans, especially in some nations, many will have heart attacks, some will have brain damage. There are some who will lose the will to live. A decision is going to be made and it will be a World-wide command/decree. It will shake the entire world and it will not be contested. This is when we will see the true Christians of the century. It will spark a worldwide war which will affect every nation. But true believers whether they live or die, their souls will be saved. God will give us the grace to stand fast by His word; and when things reach an alarming height, those in authority will propose some kind of drug to silence those who are badly affected. Places of pleasure and amusement will become as nothing. Mighty men and women will fall from their haughty lifestyles and this is the beginning of earth's sorrows especially those who turn their backs on God. The un-Godly lifestyle and those who promote it will soon drink from the bitter cup which will be poured out on the earth and they will reap what they have sown.

God is calling sinners to repent from evil before it's too late. There is a way of escape – those who call upon will be saved. Jesus died and shed His blood for mankind. (Psalm 7: 11; Psalm 9: 17)

All unsaved persons, the Lord is pleading with you to give your lives to Him right now. The Lord is calling back the backsliders; the Lord is about to remove many coverings.

# THE PROPHETIC WORD OF THE LORD
September 28, 2017
5:00 p.m.

*The Prophetic utterances of the Lord given through Apostle Dr. Steve Lyston, Bishop Dr. Doris Hutchinson, Pastor Dr. Michelle Lyston and Prophetess Sophia DiMuccio*

## Entertainment Industry

1. Dwindling and shaking will take place in the entertainment industry in general.

2. There is going to be an explosion in the Gospel Music Industry – exposure is looming over the promoters, show hosts managers and those gospel music artists that have, through their decisions and actions, caused many to shift their focus from the holiness and majesty of God and have caused people to no longer fear the Lord, but have instead reduced Him in their eyes as equal and common. God is not pleased.

3. The Lord says He is going to deal with very prominent gospel artists very strongly, very harshly because He gave them a great and significant opportunity to win a generation for Him, but they did not sit under the processing He had for them and they followed the wrong flow, and as a result there are many whose souls are at risk because of their selfishness and poor choices; they allowed the spirits

of Jezebel and Mammon to lead them instead of following His instructions.

**Jamaica**

1. The Government of Jamaica needs to establish a Prayer Center and pay those Christians who are not working to pray around the clock against disasters that would impact other nations and pray for those already affected by disasters. As they obey, God will bless the nations mightily. The Private Sector also needs to be a part of this initiative.

2. The oppression on the people of Jamaica is great! Many are crying out for change; and the Lord says "Yes! Change is coming!" The Lord also wants the parliamentarians to get closer to the people, and listen to the problems of the people, then carry out an assessment of what is needed in each household, and give assistance where needed.

3. The Lord wants the Prime Minister to call the nation into a day of prayer and fasting before it is too late – to stop the crime and violence. By obeying, great changes will come to the nation!

4. The Holy Spirit says He shall visit the Blue Mountains in Jamaica – because many evil acts are taking place there.

5. The authorities need to start putting laws in place to have mandatory evacuations in low-lying areas and

especially in Port Royal to prevent massive loss of life.

## International

1. Pray urgently against a disaster in Aruba.

2. Something will happen coming out of Egypt that will bring great exposure. It will also bring great reform to the United Nations (UN).

3. A shaking will take place in North Korea. There will also be a great shaking in other nations. There needs to be great contingency plans in place in preparation for the many disasters that are ahead. No country is safe. These disasters will also begin to expose politicians in various regions who really don't care about the people, and the relief that they want to divert from the people.

4. Something will take place in West Germany.

5. God is bring many countries back to basics and He is using nature to speak to man and it is key for each person to listen in this season. Many are watching globally to see how different governments will handle the disasters.

6. The oceans and seas are crying out – tsunamis, tidal waves and underwater volcanic eruptions as well as typhoons are pending. (Haggai 2: 21) A shift and purging of nations are taking place as the Lord is

coming against unGodly decrees and laws and the abandonment of the poor. (Isaiah 58; Matthew 25) No one can legislate God out of the nations nor stop what He is doing. God is getting the Bride ready for the return of His Son.

7. Many of the Caribbean islands that have suffered serious damage is the result of them opening their borders for the enemy to carry out sinful acts within those regions. God is getting their attention. God says He has seen the wickedness that has been taking place in secret. Many have sold out for cash!

8. As the Lord continues to shake nations, it also is a test for both political sides in the USA to come together and give assistance to the people regarding disaster relief. The Lord says the issue of race is a distraction to widen the divide. Many behind the scenes know it is not about race.

9. More devastation is coming to the USA. The US Treasury will be pressured and drained as they will spend more money than they have ever spent in history to deal with disasters.

10. Indonesia and Paris (France) will be greatly affected by disasters and riots.

11. The Lord revealed that as the sea grows angrier, we will see waves emptying massive fishes onto dry land. This will be a sign to man.

12. Stop building homes near forests as many lives will be lost if it continues. Thousands of lives will be destroyed by fire unless they take heed.

13. Many businesspeople are shipping money away to other regions, but when they are ready for it, it will be gone!

14. October to December we will continue to see worldwide mourning. There is too much evil taking place within the earth and some of what is about to happen will baffle scientists.

15. There are laws that are being formulated to come against Christian believers. When it is released many Christians will be affected! Get ready!! Get ready!!!!

# THE WORD OF THE LORD TO CHRISTIAN MUSICIANS
**Pastor Michelle Lyston**
October 29, 2017
8:28 a.m.


There is a rising of ministers of music that God is causing to take place and they will be anointed and ordained Pastors, Apostles, and Ministers. They are required to live lives that are holy before the Lord even behind closed doors. The songs of praise and of worship that will come forth through them will be songs that reveal the heart of God. An uncommon outpouring is happening and God is giving an opportunity now to those current Christian artistes to be a part of this new move that God Himself is making – meanwhile He is allowing those who have been on the "back side of the desert" – those who have waited for years unnoticed and who stood under the processing of God – those who have been waiting on the timing of God and receiving songs and sounds of music from Him - stay in His Presence, you are about to come forth in His timing – remain humble before Him.

A shift is occurring even as we speak and instead of Christian entertainers, He – God – is preparing True Worshippers to release His sound for the end time. God is stirring and consecrating those who will be UNASHAMED and UNAFRAID to declare the Sovereignty, Majesty, Power and Awesome Omnipotence, Omnipresence and Omniscience of our God! He will bestow greatness upon them to bring TOTAL glory to His name and as they remain humble before Him and study His word, then they will increase in His Spirit daily and innumerable souls will yield to Him. Many hearts and minds will be healed and souls won for Him – God! Stay In His Presence, Stay In The Mode of Worship

There are those Christian Artistes – groups and individuals - that the Lord has been speaking to and using different circumstances to get their attention and let them know that He needs them to cut back on their tours and international performances and spend time in His Presence so that He can speak to them; because He wants to use them beyond what they currently do, to reach them beyond what they (the artistes) see. The Lord says He needs them to recognize/be reminded that they are souls before they are their fans. The Lord says that these Christian artistes can no longer just go to a performance – they need to recognize the significance of what they do and more importantly, their role as they stand before the souls the Lord is allowing them to reach. They must ensure that they are covered as they go out and ensure that their families are covered before they leave – especially the male Christian artistes. The female Christian artistes must ensure that their head covers them. All must ensure that there are genuine intercessors praying for them at all times – but especially when they are doing live performances particularly (but not only) in other nations.

Do not lay hands on everyone simply because they are there, The Lord must direct you especially in this season -

because you can get hit spiritually and be defeated by the enemy.

African, Latin and Caribbean Christian Worship and Praise music is about to rise to the fore in unprecedented ways among the general audience and move beyond the comfortable place. These Worshippers must seek to learn other languages, because the Lord is going to use them beyond those who speak their own language. God wants to take worship to another level that breaks the barriers of language and culture, and He needs all the Worshipper to be ready to do this. Some will begin to speak and understand languages that are not their native tongue. An uncommon outpouring is taking place and we must position ourselves to receive it!

# RESTORATION FOR 2018
Apostle Dr. Steve Lyston
Received December 28, 2017

As we prepare for the New Year, never mistake a blessing for the approval of God. The criteria for blessings as stated in Matthew 5: 45 *"...For He makes His sun rise on the evil and on the good, and sends rain on the just and on the unjust."* God gives grace and favor on both evil and good, just and unjust.

But what now separates us is the approval of God. You can have a big bank account, husband or wife, mega or small church; even a title; but do you have God's approval?

## God's Blessing Vs God's Approval

Moses and the Children of Israel received the blessings of God. God told Moses not to strike the rock, but instead to speak to it and Moses disobeyed. Ultimately, while Moses and the people remained blessed, his actions disqualified him from crossing over. He did not get approval to cross over.

Ensure that in pursuing prosperity God always gets the honor and glory, and that we please Him. A man's material blessing is not an indication that God is with him.

In order to know you have God's approval, you can use the word of God as our guide. Additionally, as you pray and fast, His Holy Spirit will give you the instruction and tell you how to proceed. Any instruction God gives us, the result must and will give Him glory at all times, never man. Anything that gives man glory over God profanes His name and arouses His anger. So for example, where politicians, business people or John Q. Public want to bring changes without God it always brings them into a worse situation; because no man has the ability to please man, only God can do that. A man without God can be famous with man, but He will be unpopular with God and ultimately reap that reward.

Everything a person does to get success, must first please God. It is not about a person's agenda for a nation or a household, it is about God's agenda – what He wants to accomplish; and there are many from time to time who will try to please man in the pursuit of prosperity, but in doing so they displease God. Please God and He will please everybody else.

In 2018, for those who want real success, begin to please God in your endeavors.

**Restoration**

Undoubtedly, in 2018, there will be great opportunities for those who want to be restored regardless of what they have been through, but to get restored we must allow God to do that - we must trust Him.

There are many areas in our lives that we have chosen to lock away or build a wall around because we want to leave it untouched – maybe it is an area that is very painful or that we have become comfortable living with. Sadly, many of the things that we have suffered are connected to choices that God did not approve, and that led to pain, hurt and betrayal. Subsequently, some become embittered and unforgiving. But for restoration to come, there has to be repentance first. Then there will be restitution. So such a person will now need to make some things right, apologize to those they hurt, return anything they took that did not belong to them so that they can be restored.

Thereafter there will be revival and refreshing, and they will see the obstacles and hindrance move and there will be a new opportunity to move forward – in health, finance, relationships and all other areas. Furthermore there will be elevation/promotion. Full joy will be restored.

Your restoration is important, because as you are restored, other people, will then be restored. When Esther, Joseph, Ruth, Naomi and Job were restored, it impacted the lives of many others. Other people are waiting on your restoration. Don't let anyone convince that there is a job shortage or money shortage. What we have is a distribution problem – often times the wrong people are in position and so they distribute to those of like mind. Never tell God how to restore you. The restoration of the four (4) lepers brought about the restoration of an entire city. (2 Kings 6 – 7). God is looking for people with faith to believe in Him. Always remember that faith demands action. You cannot have faith and sit in one place. When you move by faith, God always meets your faith. There are many Christians that put limits on God. Some even want to give up. Some are looking at things on the natural level – looking at their situations and believing that nothing can change.

With God all things are possible and if you believe it you will receive it.

# 2018

# THE PROPHETIC WORD OF THE LORD FOR 2018 AND ONWARD

*Through Prophetess Doris Hutchinson, Apostle Steve Lyston, Prophetess Michelle Lyston, Prophetess Sophia DiMuccio, Prophetess Nadra Brotherton, Prophet O. Onesto Jolly, Prophet David Benoit.*

The number 5778 and the number 2018 signify grace, completion, new beginnings, births, deaths, spiritual perfection, redemption, rest and blessings, a holy time, freedom, jubilee, circumcision of the flesh, the government of God. 2018 is the year of reckoning, shock and awe! For 2018, many of the rich will begin to cry out for mercy from God because of the various things they shall encounter. The Lord is speaking to His People everywhere to be ready for His Return. Things will be very unpredictable, and it will be a mixed year. Many plans that are in place for 2018, whether good or bad will be disrupted drastically. Many longstanding companies will disappear.

As such, God says He will not accept a double standard life from believers as He requires holiness. Too many of His people pretend and live a double lifestyle. The Lord says He will lift a standard. As His people live holy, then one shall chase a thousand and two will put ten thousand to flight. (Joshua 23: 10)

In 2018 many will be released from bondage, while many others will fall away in bondage and deception. Luke 13: 16, Judges 3: 14 and Judges 10: 7 - 8. We will see the shaking of world systems: industrial, economic and Godless commercialism and religious, as more countries will begin to align with the anti-Christ system. There will be famine and water shortages in some countries, while more floods, fire and earthquakes will continue in other areas; and civil war will break out.

Frightening new laws will decreed globally in 2018, and the Lord said his people should look up as redemption draws nigh. We will see shaking and shifting in every sector in 2018. We will see more signs that will physically and spiritually be manifested in the sky. But the Lord says his people should prepare for a great harvest of souls that are coming home in 2018. Watch out for the word vortex.

Plagues and sicknesses will breakout but there will be a mighty revival of the Holy Spirit in 2018. Revelation 18:3-6 (KJV)

"For all nations have drunk of the wine of the wrath of her fornication, and the kings of the earth have committed fornication with her, and the merchants of the earth are waxed rich through the abundance of her delicacies. And I heard another voice from heaven, saying, Come out of her, my people, that ye be not partakers of her sins, and that ye receive not of her plagues. For her sins have reached unto heaven, and God hath remembered her iniquities. Reward her even as she rewarded you, and double unto her double according to her works: in the cup which she hath filled fill to her double."

1. A great change is coming worldwide. All nations that will not cease to worship idols will experience another wave of disasters. For the Lord says He will visit and dismantle places of amusement wherein evil takes place. The stench of sin has come up before God and unless they repent they will all likewise perish.

2. The global media is doing great harm to life and the population of the earth. And because of their doing, the media will suffer greatly. The action of the media is hurting the future generations and the hands of the Lord will be heavy upon them in 2018.

3. There will be widespread divorce in 2018 going forward. Wives and husbands who want their marriages to be safe should tell their spouses to be truthful to them before it is too late, and that if they continue to hide their lifestyle, things will become worse and there will be a great separation which will have a significant effect on businesses, friendships, churches and children. This is the time all married couples should get before God and rededicate their lives so they can be examples to the younger generation or else, the younger generation will become worse than this one is currently.

4. The entire earth is about to experience a shift like we have never seen before. We will be seeing a significant number of shifts that will affect political leadership locally and globally. Priorities will also shift, but with all that will be happening, there will be

mighty outpouring from God's Spirit upon vessels taking place at the same time.

## Jamaica

5. There will be a major upset in the political system in Jamaica. If systems are left unchecked, there will be hacking on both sides and they will be digging up a lot of 'dirt' on each other like we have never seen before – even banking information; and it will spark another wave of murders. Look out also for disgruntled workers that have been/will be let go, exposing company information – both in public and private sector.

6. Jamaica has been given a new lease on mercy, but the actions of the people of Jamaica determines what happens next. It is the last chance that He is giving to Jamaica before He makes His move. Jamaica is on probation.

7. A massive financial scandal is going to hit the nation. Many will be exposed.

8. The Lord is calling all the church leaders in Jamaica to repent. Many of them cannot see beyond the money. "Repent, before the Lord removes your candlestick."

9. 6 Major happenings will hit Jamaica and it will shake the core of the nation.

10. Pray for the protection and the life of the Prime Minister and also of the opposition also.

11. There is major trouble ahead within the nation. The spirit of the supplanting will rise within each political party. Many of the politicians have aligned themselves with different foreign powers and foreign agencies to give them power and this will have serious repercussions.

12. Play for the electoral system in Jamaica as there are serious plans and problems ahead.

13. Pray for the opposition party in Jamaica. More of them will have health issues and will have to leave.

14. In all of this, purging will be taking place within Jamaica. A new nation will rise. We shall truly see the nation become "Out of Many One People."

15. A new leadership shall emerge that will follow God's instructions and will have a heart for the poor the fatherless and the widow. Jamaica belongs to God and He will get the nation where He wants it. For the Lord said that the problem that the nation is going through is the result of the hands of so many of the leaders of the nation (past and present) being covered with the blood of the innocent and they refuse

to repent. The Lord says that the remnant should not cease to intercede that the eyes of the people will open to see the truth.

16. The Lord has been warning Jamaica and the leaders of the nation to seek Him before certain laws are passed but they consistently ignore Him. Many of the laws passed will affect the country negatively and Jamaica will become poorer, physically and spiritually. Investments will go down and there will be a terrible cry in Jamaica. The nation will not know who to trust as many have been undermining the country in order to prosper at the expense of the nation. But the Lord will shake their financial foundation. The poor and the less fortunate have been crying and no one listened and because of the frustration and bewilderment, they will now go after the rich. Many empty promises have been given, but God has heard their cry. The Lord says He shall raise up an army of men and women with an end-time message. Many who have turned their backs on the Lord shall not escape the judgement. The Lord says, "I have warned the land but they have not heeded. Grievous wolves have crept in the land and many are not able to discern them. These wolves plan to drain the nations' finances and many will come begging for crumbs. Many innocent lives have been lost because of what they know, and for many

others, if they speak they will be taken out secretly.

17. A great and shocking exposure is coming to the nation and many will hide themselves away. But the Lord says the faithful must continue, because a great revival is coming. Prepare yourselves.

18. There will be a stirring within the Jamaican Police Force – unrest is brewing. Undermining is about to be exposed and even greater exposure is ahead. One very popular member of the police force is about to get an awakening and the Lord is going to open his eyes and show him many things. God will give him boldness. (It is not time for "Bigga" Ford to retire.)

19. There are persons who will be leaving their jobs at the Office of the Prime Minister/Jamaica House.

20. There is a secret cry taking place because of what is happening within the nation. Leaders have been operating with two laws in effect – one for the rich and another for the poor. Many turn their eyes to the evil. But the Lord says He is going to do something in the nation that is going to tickle many ears. Many have stocked away finances, while ignoring the cry for help

from the people and many know what has been done to spike the crime rates.

21. God says He is going to expose the evil of the land, and many will see His handiwork. We will see kingdoms come down suddenly.

22. God shall visit the different hills in Jamaica. Many will be exposed and many will know who the problem is in Jamaica. Politics, business, security and Churchmen. Some fearless youth will rise up in the area of politics and many seasoned politicians will be moved out of place. Watch the hands of the Lord.

23. The Lord says He has been warning Jamaica to pull out of and avoid any additional loans from international lenders because He knows their motives. Their goal is to strip the nation. The structure of some of their agreements is of such that the interest on these loans will bring greater burden and severe hardship on the nation and its people. There is great suffering ahead unless some of these loans are re-negotiated in favor of the people. Be warned, many of these loans are traps!

24. Racism will rise in Jamaica's private and public

organizations. Many will be overlooked for employment and promotions because of the color of their skin.

25. The Spirit of the Lord says He is not pleased with the Leader of this nation, as well as with the other Politicians because they have turned their backs on His instructions.

26. Thus Saith the Lord to Christians, "Awake from your slumber!" "Arise from your sleep!" "Weep and Mourn for Your Nation, for My Eyes have seen to and fro throughout this land and My Judgment is upon this Nation, says the Lord

27. The Lord is about to expose more prominent spiritual leaders who have been living different lifestyles that will break the spirit of deception that has been blinding the eyes of the people.

28. The murder rate in Jamaica can be reduced, but there are well-known ex-politicians who have been contributing to the majority of the crimes committed. A sudden attack will be upon those who behind the crime and violence locally and internationally. Many elite will be exposed.

29. The Lord will expose persons within the health sector who have been misdiagnosing patients, especially small children and seniors through the administering of certain medications who end up with terminal illnesses. The Lord says many of these practitioners will lose their medical licenses for malpractice.

30. There are more financial mergers concerning banks that will occur because of misappropriation of funds.

31. Jamaica will face tough decisions regarding their allegiance to larger nations particularly in the area of laws and regulations being passed. The Lord says Jamaica's leaders need to seek Him as their source before making decisions hastily. Their decisions have the potential to negatively impact the nation and to cause problems at the diplomatic level. It is critical for Jamaica to make the right decisions.

32. The Spirit of the Lord says He is displeased with the growing number of homeless persons across the island who need urgent spiritual, medical, emotional and financial attention, who at some point been rejected by society, but He says they belong to Him and He did not come for the righteous, but for those who are sick (spiritually

and naturally), and this exposes the hearts of Christians, especially spiritual leaders. They are about their own business, except taking care of His business and His business takes precedence over everything.

33. The Spirit of the Lord says there is much work to be done within different churches, especially traditional churches where people are not healed and delivered (not set free). These churches are mostly concerned about the monies coming in and the people are dying spiritually - no training, just making up numbers.

34. The Spirit of the Lord says the Jamaican Government will institute more laws that will cause spiritual and natural oppression upon the people, but there will be a set of people who will be brave, will not compromise and fight for the Perfect Will of the Lord to be established.

35. The Year 2018 will bring about a lot of rebellion, persecutions and bondage that will cause major revolutions to take place.

36. The Entertainment Industry in Jamaica is in serious trouble - entertainers will be turning against each other and it will cause many to look UP!

37. There are prominent schools in Kingston that are experiencing financial problems and health issues and will be forced to close down. Pray for those schools.

38. A new rise of athletes will emerge and take on the sports arena by storm.

39. The orphanages nationwide need much attention spiritually, medically and financially and educationally.

40. There is a rise of incest within families, especially among children, but these children are bribed so as not to speak out against these evil. They are even told that nothing is wrong and it is acceptable because cousins sleep with cousins within the royal family and nobody squeals about that. But, the Lord is about to intercept and destroy this deceptive demon.

41. There are many people who are asking for the return of Jamaica's National Fleet - Air Jamaica and for more access to be granted with different Hubs worldwide and this Fleet still has much favor with God. The Lord says someone needs to come forward and bid to bring it back. It will bring great blessing to the nation.

42. There will be more Latinos visiting Jamaica's

Soil because of its rich heritage and similarities with a few Hispanic countries.

43. It is time for all Politicians to speak the truth concerning their ingenuity towards the people because each of them will stand before God on Judgment Day to give an account to Him for their lies and deception practices.

44. If both the government and the opposition don't revisit their advisors and the advice they are getting to move the country forward, the outcomes will be frightening, because many of the advisors are in it to advance their own cause and they are not functioning in the interest of the nation.

45. The Spirit of the Lord says each household need to set their houses in order for Jesus Christ is coming again! Who hath an ear, hear what the Spirit of the Lord is saying.

46. The Spirit of the Lord says the Agricultural Industry in Jamaica is in for troubled times because of the increase of natural disasters that will greatly affect the soil.

47. The watchmen in Jamaica are sleeping! Arise! Arise out of your slumber and travail for the land. Weep for the nation! Blow the trumpet

and keep silent no more," says the Spirit of the Living God!

48. There are going to be riots breaking out in certain parts of Jamaica, and this will bring the leaders to their knees because of continuous disobedience and rebellion over many years.

49. The Lord is calling all Christians in Jamaica to discern, especially now to His Return, for there are many hirelings, cults and some leaders are involved in debauchery - living multiple lifestyles. This had scattered much of His sheep. Thus saith the Lord, "Beware of wolves in sheep's clothing, for they are many," saith GOD!

50. A religious deception will hit Jamaica. The people need to be watchful. The Lord says they should study the word as never before and pray as never before. There will be strong delusions

51. Jamaica is now standing at a cross roads, the question will be asked: what next do they have to present to the people. All leaders in Jamaica need to examine their role within the society for the eyes of the Lord are watching Jamaica. Those in charge must take responsibility for the growth and success and the spiritual life of the country for the Lord says it is no longer business as usual.

52. The spirit of Eli has taken over many of the church leaders in Jamaica and they are about to be called into accountability by God. The Glory of God is about to depart for them and their cry will be great; because there have been many warnings going out to them, but they have refused to renew their minds. They now stand in God's way and resist Him and everything He desires to do. The Lord says their time has come and there will be a sudden shake and shift!

53. The Lord has seen the faithful remnant. There are some churches and leaders that have been pressing despite great oppositions. You have stood and suffered great persecution. Continue to stand. God is about to promote you because of your faithfulness. Remember, do not walk the way of those before you who became unfaithful, proud and disobedient. The Lord says remain humble as He lifts you up and you will eat the fruit of the land and receive His reward.

54. There are some organizations with limited resources that have been doing a great deal to help the youth. The Lord says He sees all that you do and He is pleased. However, He says be careful not to become corrupt when He begins to open doors for you.

55. The Lord says the shaking that is about to take

place on the political scene is going to be so severe that the churches in Jamaica will need to pray for a new generation of leaders to rise up who will not compromise and will look to God to bring the change needed within the nation. Those who will not bow to corrupt organizations or seek to destroy the nation. The Lord says, "The shaking will be great My people but do not be surprised."

56. The Lord says that the intercessors within the nation must not get caught up in politically driven intercession, nor should five-fold leaders be engaged in politically-driven actions and decision-making. The Lord says, do not allow His name to be profaned. Stand in integrity.

## Globally

57. Globally, things will become very serious, that even famous and historical landmarks will be utterly destroyed. So if people don't change the way they think and operate, we will see suicide rate will increase to a level we have never seen before. Watch Taj Mahal and other historic and protected places globally. Some of these happenings will be frightening. The Lord is going to visit the temple monks as a sign that Jesus is coming.

58. Focus on Revelation 5, Revelation 8, and Revelation 18. We are going to see a lot of problems with the cosmos (cosmic convulsions) similar to Exodus 10: 21 – as a sign of God's displeasure in the earth. There will be a lot of activity on/with the sun and scientists will have their hands full. There will be problems with vegetation as well as volcanic eruptions, increase of earthquakes in diverse places and serious problems with marine life. May fish will die and there will be great pollution. Meteors will fall and there will be increased testing of weapons in the sea. (Joel 2: 30 – 32, Jeremiah 9: 15 – 23). All these things will affect crop, property and life. We will be seeing greater flooding, more bloodshed and pestilence.

59. Many nations will now rise up against Israel like never before and will join in a coalition against the state of Israel. They will have secret meetings, and coerce other nations to join in the fight against Israel. Watch Germany, Russia and France among other countries.

60. We must pray for Israel. There will be Nations which will be redeemed in relationships with Israel, the church and Jerusalem. There will be great persecution of the church in 2018, all eyes

will also be on the church in 2018. All eyes will be on Israel and we will see the awakening power of the bride and the bridegroom coming together out of the wilderness.

61. Many earthly governments will experience collapse. The Lord shall expose many prominent Politicians around the World, especially USA, France, Switzerland, Norway, Uganda, Germany, India, Pakistan, China, South Korea, Grenada and Dominica. Also, the people in New Delhi India are crying out for economic change and they are willing to demonstrate for this change to come forth now. Furthermore, the Prime Minister for Germany will institute three new laws that will affect its neighboring countries. The Spirit of the Lord says that it is time for accountability from the Leaders worldwide, for His judgment is sure, and He is not mocked!

62. Three (3) world leaders will be going down and suffer defeat in 2018. Also, the most powerful world leader will have mixed thoughts about walking away from his responsibilities. No one knows the depths of the pain that he has in his heart because of the responsibility. The Lord says the people must pray for stability

63. There will be wars in the ocean. Many problems

will arise in the oceans which can cause major losses. Especially with tuna fish. Many who eat tuna fish will get sick because of ocean contamination

64. Many plagues are going to break out on those who practice witchcraft, sexual immorality and those who rob the poor. (Revelation 9: 21; Revelation 16). There are going to be a lot of skin diseases happening because the kingdom of Heaven is at hand and God is warning His people to be ready.

65. Pray for Pastor Joel Osteen and his family. There will also be a mighty purging of the cardinals in the Vatican.

66. There is a spiritual explosion that is about to happen within the USA that will cause many to scatter seeking for new church and for some it will deter them from finding a church home. "Because of lack of knowledge, My people perish. Many have gone back to the beggarly elements. I am preparing you My people, to go back into the harvest field to reap the harvest," says the Lord.

67. Many US soldiers will be court marshalled for hacking into classified documents.

68. A lot of controversy will surround the Royal

Family as Prince Harry and his fiancée approach their wedding day.

69. The Spirit of the Lord says there needs to be more attention placed upon children everywhere (globally) who are neglected (rejected) and without shelter and food.

70. Homelessness will increase within the US by 80%

71. There will be weeping and wailing throughout the country. Many will be coming under great stress and will flee to the Appalachian Mountains. There are more forest fires expected to burn in California that will force some of the people to reside in other states. More floods and disasters will continue to hit the world. There will be more natural disasters worldwide in the forms of tsunamis, earthquakes and hurricanes. Pray for all means of transportation and protection of the people.

72. Nations need to be ready to assist other nations because a chemical disaster is at large. Many seas are going to be polluted due to rebellion in man throughout the ecosystem. I saw in the Spirit as if the extinct of Dolphins due to severe pollution. Due to the severe pollution that will be taking place, many will become infected

from every class level. However, the poor will be more susceptible to the health hazards.

73. 6 states in the USA will suffer greatly. Cease your fighting among each other Republicans and Democrats. You are walking in pride, and I hate a proud look. Prepare your hearts – I will pour out fresh anointing this is your season. More exposures are coming for both the Democratic and Republican Parties - many will be forced to hand in their resignations

74. Pray for the continent of Africa. There will be more disasters, murders and killings. Spend time in My presence. Wait on Me until you hear Me. Also in 2018 watch Egypt, Syria, Greece, Italy, Iraq, Iran, China, Russia, Turkey and USA

75. Fire will burn in diverse places in America, Africa, and West of Indonesia.

76. The Lord is taking down those of the rich who extort the poor, so that some of them will sit down at the doorsteps of the poor and be seeking help from them, but some will be seeking help to be rich again quickly.

77. Kentucky and Texas are going to get hit with

disasters.

78. It may seem as if some of the African nations have not been touched, however, many of them will experience worse. There is an evil that exists in Nigeria that is worse than what we have seen before, and it will be exposed.

79. There is restlessness within the US police force. Racism within is causing the divide to widen. Pray for the Police Force throughout the United States.

80. There will be a wave of different prejudices coming to the fore across the world to bring division among race, color, ethnic, language and tongue.

81. More will go from the White House.

82. We will see cyber-electronic devices, IDs and other data driven systems that will be implemented under the guise of boosting national security and bringing economic growth to countries, but the Lord says be ready my people.

83. There will be major breakthroughs in medicine. However, the discrimination regarding who gets help will be very evident.

84. New laws will be put in place to oppress the

Church, and these will be implemented under the guise of the inter-faith - read Revelation 12

85. For the Lord said, "A lot of evil will be exposed by the end of this year and into the next year. This is a warning as God is not pleased. He has given many warnings, and many have not heeded. As exposure takes place, things will become worse. Therefore, all Christians need to live holy lives and all unsaved persons need to repent and turn their lives to Him now. For the Lord says as He exposes the evil and the evil plans, especially in some nations, many will have heart attacks, some will have brain damage. There are some who will lose the will to live. A decision is going to be made and it will be a World-wide command/decree. It will shake the entire world and it will not be contested. This is when we will see the true Christians of the century. It will spark a worldwide war which will affect every nation. But true believers whether they live or die, their souls will be saved. God will give us the grace to stand fast by His word; and when things reach an alarming height, those in authority will propose some kind of drug to silence those who are badly affected.

86. Places of pleasure and amusement will become as nothing. Mighty men and women will fall from their haughty lifestyles and this is the beginning of earth's sorrows especially those

who turn their backs on God. The un-Godly lifestyle and those who promote it will soon drink from the bitter cup which will be poured out on the earth and they will reap what they have sown.

87. The Lord is calling upon Capitol Hill, United States of America to humble come before the Lord, both democrats and republicans, and seek Him for the Nation and the unity of the Nation. They are spending too much time plotting against each other while the nation is suffering. For the Lord said, "Nothing is hidden form Him, God." God is going to show a sign in Capitol Hill that is going to bring everyone to their knees. And they will know the power of God.

88. Urgent cry out for the country of Uganda. As there is a plot to overthrow the government. Christians need to cry out that Uganda won't plunge into chaos. There will be a restructuring within the Government of Uganda-Democratic

89. Their needs to be a united effort to deal with the
refugee crisis. Nations and Member states need to re-negotiate the Preamble of the 1951 Convention on Refugees. There is going to be a heavy influx of refugees that will be running for their lives to Hawaii, USA, and to some European nations. We need to pray for them.

90. to  Pray for the United Nations. Crises will begin hit globally, and they will be caught off guard. What is written on paper is not what is taking place on the ground. The United Nations needs to get back to the original mandate, or which when they were first establish, International Peace, security, and economics issues. This will lead to many resignations. God needs them to seek Him and seek His people for spiritual guidance. Without a revelation the people perish. There are growing issues within the United Nations that will be made public.

91. Pray that global world leaders will put plan in place in the event of famine that will hit the globe. In particular, health, food, and shelter; storage and logistics.

92. A popular World Leader will be leaving the scene.

93. I saw in the Spirit as it were a decision the President of the USA made this year within the economic sector that will shock the WORLD. Pray also for USA Politician, Paul R. Leonard and for his health

94. The Lord says the US government is about to experience serious, heavily influential and manipulative forces and undermining that will

affect polices, and state governance. We must pray against ulterior motives hidden under good morals. Many women and men will be appointed to positions of power and great influence, but their motives are less than wholesome and dangerous to the Christian faith and to the country.

95. The Lord says the gates within the nation must be guarded – the churches, private sector, the government (Federal, state, and local). Whatever the church allows to slip through could be the beginning of the end.

96. Christian leaders who are counselors/advisors to the President and Governors in the USA, God says you're are asleep and need to be awakened. He is going to shift you out and shift in true watchmen that are vigilant and sensitive to the Holy Spirit; those who will not be afraid to speak what God is actually saying.

**Body Of Christ**

97. Acts 3 – This is a time of refreshing. Do not leave my presence until you receive the refreshing. The time for signs and wonders are here. Are you ready to receive that anointing? I will be pouring it out.

98. All five-fold ministries that are functioning for and focused on fame and power, God will visit with them. Many are not living holy, for the

Lord says, they have not hallowed His name, nor are they pleasing Him. He says they must remember Matthew 7: 22 – 23.

99. The Lord says his people should study carefully the book of revelation, in particular, Revelation 11 and Revelation 17. We also see the manifestation and the emergence of the apostate church (falling stars)

100. How many are willing to go – India, Africa, China, and Russia are calling. The Caribbean also. Many of you have lost your zeal. Saith the Lord, I will visit you and pull you out of your comfort zone. I will make the provision for you to go. Come before me and seek me. Many have fallen before Me behind closed doors. I see your lifestyle. Are you ready to go into the world? I have sent you and you have not gone. Are you ready? I am preparing you to go into the mission field. Many will go from country to country with missionaries to reap the harvest. All true believers prepare yourself! This is the time of the great outpouring of the Holy Spirit. (Joel 2:28) the harvest is ripe.

101. Many call My name and lift their hands but their hearts are not with Me. Some of the ministers are not living right. "Walk upright and holy before Me! I have seen your deeds – they are not hidden. I shall expose your doings if you do not turn from your wicked ways" says

the Lord. He has called them together to renew their vows and consecrate them. Some have other women with their wives. I am now ready, says God, to pour into you and renew your vows. Many have gone after filthy lucre, but I will abundantly pardon. The Lord says He is going to refill and renew them.

102. The time for change has come. Many have no example to follow that is why the unsaved behave the way they do. A great revival will break out locally and globally and no one should try to hinder God's work. For the Lord says, it is time for the people to stop worshipping idols and serve the true and living God -apostles, evangelists, prophets will be chosen and sent to many nations. God is now ready to forgive, cleanse, wash, purge, renew and bless!

103. A wind of change is coming. God wants to restore leaders and all of us to a more dedicated life of working for Him. Be faithful, trustworthy, holy, loving and caring toward each other. We are His voice on earth. Therefore, our lifestyle must be pleasing to Him.

104. God is getting ready to purge the churches. Many will be leaving, but many more will be coming in as they leave. Shepherds need to

guard the flock as grievous wolves will be rising up.

105. The Lord says, "Another Step" He is calling the Body of Christ to take another step of Faith, another step of Holiness, another step of readiness because the rapture can be anytime. Another step of Soul-winning.

106. John 10 – this is the season of exposure. The true shepherds versus wolves and hirelings and false sheep. In the same way that we have false sheep. True sheep know the true shepherd's voice. False sheep follow false shepherds. If they were true, they would have a desire for the Word. True sheep stay in God's presence and study His word and will not be easily deceived. There is great deception coming. The true heart will know His voice while the false hear will follow others. We will see the rise of the Pharisees because they were not true sheep.

107. God is calling His people to a place of intimacy with Him, so that He can speak to His people as there is serious deception ahead.

108. The Lord says take note of Psalm 33: 10 – 12 which says "The Lord brings the counsel of the nations to nothing; He makes the plans of the peoples of no effect. The counsel of the Lord stands forever, the plans of His heart to all generations. Blessed is the nation whose God is

the Lord, the people He has chosen as His own inheritance" Note also Proverbs 19: 21 which reminds us, "There are many plans in a man's heart, nevertheless the Lord's counsel—that will stand."

109. Something is about to happen worldwide that will wake up the Body of Christ and cause a united move in the right direction.

110. "Many true prophets of God are about to be persecuted as the prophet Jeremiah was persecuted. Are you ready for change that is coming? Who is on the Lord's side?" The Lord is speaking more in this very hour. "Who has ears to hear, let him hear what the Spirit of the Lord is saying," says the Lord. For God is about to break the backs of all nation leaders because He is about to manifest in ways we have not seen before, and it will pass on from one generation to the next.

**Christian Musicians**

111. There is a rising of ministers of music that God is causing to take place and they will be anointed and ordained Pastors, Apostles, and Ministers. They are required to live lives that are holy before the Lord even behind closed doors. The songs of praise and of worship that will come forth through them will be songs that

reveal the heart of God. An uncommon outpouring is happening and God is giving an opportunity now to those current Christian artistes to be a part of this new move that God Himself is making – meanwhile He is allowing those who have been on the "back side of the desert" – those who have waited for years unnoticed and who stood under the processing of God – those who have been waiting on the timing of God and receiving songs and sounds of music from Him - stay in His Presence, you are about to come forth in His timing – remain humble before Him.

112. A shift is occurring even as we speak and instead of Christian entertainers, He – God – is preparing True Worshippers to release His sound for the end time. God is stirring and consecrating those who will be Unashamed and Unafraid to declare the Sovereignty, Majesty, Power and Awesome Omnipotence, Omnipresence and Omniscience of our God! He will bestow greatness upon them to bring TOTAL glory to His name and as they remain humble before Him and study His word, then they will increase in His Spirit daily and innumerable souls will yield to Him. Many hearts and minds will be healed and souls won for Him – God!

113. There are those Christian Artistes – groups

and individuals - that the Lord has been speaking to and using different circumstances to get their attention and let them know that He needs them to cut back on their tours and international performances and spend time in His Presence so that He can speak to them; because He wants to use them beyond what they currently do, to reach them beyond what they (the artistes) see. The Lord says He needs them to recognize/be reminded that they are souls before they are their fans.

114. The Lord says that these Christian artistes can no longer just go to a performance – they need to recognize the significance of what they do and more importantly, their role as they stand before the souls the Lord is allowing them to reach. They must ensure that they are covered as they go out and ensure that their families are covered before they leave – especially the male Christian artistes. The female Christian artistes must ensure that their head covers them. All must ensure that there are genuine intercessors praying for them at all times – but especially when they are doing live performances particularly (but not only) in other nations.

115. Do not lay hands on everyone simply because they are there, The Lord must direct you especially in this season - because you can get hit spiritually and be defeated by the enemy.

116. African, Latin and Caribbean Christian Worship and Praise music is about to rise to the fore in unprecedented ways among the general audience and move beyond the comfortable place. These Worshippers must seek to learn other languages, because the Lord is going to use them beyond those who speak their own language. God wants to take worship to another level that breaks the barriers of language and culture and He needs all the Worshipper to be ready to do this. Some will begin to speak and understand languages that are not their native tongue. An uncommon outpouring is taking place and we must position ourselves to receive it!

117. The Lord is calling upon Christian entertainers to ensure that souls, prayer and feeding of the poor must be the priority; and there must be unity like never before.

## Entertainers/VIPs

118. Pray for the following sports persons:

- Usain Bolt – that he will give his life to the Lord. Pray for his parents' health also.
- Indian cricketer Sachin Tendulkar.
- W.I. Cricketers Courtney Walsh and Brian Lara. Pray for their health and their

economic well-being and that they will come to the Lord fully.

119. Pray for the following Hollywood stars:

- Robyn Rihanna Fenty,
- Mariah Carey,
- Gabrielle Union – she needs to be careful of the roles she accepts, (and pray for her husband Dwayne Wade).
- Oprah Winfrey
- Moses Davis (Beenie Man) Time is running out. The Lord wants him now!

120. Pray for Serena Williams and her family.
Beyonce and Jay-Z will encounter many accusations that will test their marriage as never before. More shaking will take place in Hollywood. The Lord needs Tiger Woods' full attention because it is time for him to surrender to Him totally for he is chosen to preach God's Word and that they all will come and know the true and living God.

*The Prophecies given are for 2018 onward. God can choose to hold His hand back from any form of judgement pending, subject to the repentance of nations and individuals. Jonah 3: 5—10; Exodus 32: 14; Jeremiah 18: 7—11; Amos 7: 3—6; II Kings 20: 1—11 and I Corinthians 13: 9. Please remember, God does whatever He pleases (Psalm 135: 6). He changes Times and Seasons; He removes kings and raises up kings (Daniel 1: 20—23).*

# THE PROPHETIC WORD OF THE LORD

## March 20, 2018

*Through Apostle Steve Lyston, Prophetess Doris Hutchinson and Prophetess Sophia DiMuccio.*

## Jamaica

1. Urgent prayer for the Jamaica Baptist Union and the leader.

2. Pray for Pearnel Charles.

3. Prayer for Forest Hills, Arnett Gardens. Shores Hill. The authorities need to be vigilant in those areas.

4. There is a trap set for a popular clergyman regarding sexual misconduct.

5. The Bureau of Standards needs to examine in greater detail, the lighters and matches that are being imported. Many are defective and can cause unexpected fires.

6. Many pastors in Jamaica have diverted from the straight path. Many are now involved in the occult with regard to getting wealth and position, and their souls are in danger.

7. Pray for all the former Prime Ministers.

8. The Lord says that the crime problem in Jamaica is deeper than we think. God says His people need to go deeper for Him to show the root problem. The crime problem is directly related to the direction of the nation and power. Pray that there will be a major exposure. It will bring tears to many Jamaicans because God says He has seen the plans and the plots, and He has also seen what takes place in the sea. Also, while many may be focusing on the men involved in criminal activities, there are many women who are the driving force behind them. Pray that they will be exposed.

9. God says big men are behind the crime and He is about to remove 2 of them. The Lord says watch His hand at work. Two (2) top men will go down.

10. There is a plan to unite the gunmen to carry out attacks. The nation must pray!!!

11. A terrible exposure will take place and Jamaica will be delivered.

12. A major probe will take place regarding the tourist industry in Jamaica.

## Globally

13. Serious prayer needed for the US Army. Many of them are wrongly positioned and their lives will be lost if they don't change their strategies.

14. Christians need to cry out for America. They also need to pray for the homeless as many more are about to become homeless this year.

15. A great purging and a great deception is about to

    hit the world, particularly among the youth.

16. Pray regarding a possible conflict between Jordan and the USA. Wisdom is needed in terms of dealing with or responding certain situations.

17. Pray for global economic exposure that involves

    Switzerland. Many politicians will get caught up in it.

18. Pray for Guyana – against earthquakes and a potential tsunami

19. Pray for Senator Ted Cruz.

20. Pray for the US President – President Donald Trump.

21. A great deal of money will be spent on all those who leave his Administration for them to speak to the media.

22. Pray for all the stadiums in the USA especially the one in Miami, Florida.

23. Pray for the salvation of Arnold Schwarzenegger that he will surrender to the Lord. He will be experiencing the supernatural.

## Entertainment

24. Julio Iglesias, Diana Ross and Bruce Springsteen have weathered many storms in their lives, but this is the time for them to give their lives to the Lord – now!

25. Pray also for Montel Williams. God loves and cares for him and he must know that God is his personal Savior.

# THE PROPHETIC WORD OF THE LORD
## May 18, 2018

*(Through Apostle Dr. Steve Lyston, Bishop Dr. Doris Hutchinson, and Prophetess Sophia DiMuccio)*

It is critical for us to understand the Times and Seasons – what to do and how to prepare. We are now seeing a global shifting and shaking take place and the Wind of the Spirit is blowing to bring great exposure and shatter many plans that are contrary to God's plans and purpose.

We must pray for our children as the enemy wants an assault launched against the children to destroy them. So the Lord wants parents to rise up and take a stand.

Thus says the Lord: There shall be a great turmoil in the east that cannot be quenched by man-made tools, because it is My perfect will. Also there will be weeping and wailing from the west. My wrath will be upon the following nations:

- Turkey
- Saudi Arabia
- Eastern Europe
- Palestine
- Pakistan
- Uzbekistan
- Egypt
- Iran
- USA especially Massachusetts and Kentucky.

There will be many uprisings within the USA:

- New York
- North Carolina
- South Carolina
- West Virginia
- Washington D.C.
- Florida
- Alabama

**Jamaica**

There will be a lot of demonstrations taking place in Jamaica; particularly in the vicinity of the Jamaica House.

Pray for a former, very vocal security minister.

The crime in Jamaica is well orchestrated with a greater motive behind it. If it is successful in achieve its goals then there will be a switch and it will be too late by the time the people of Jamaica's eyes open, it will be too late. There needs to be closer monitoring of all airlines coming into the country – publicly or privately. The airports need to tighten up their security at the airports.

Great exposure will take place in the financial sector. It is about land and other resources. The global and local media will begin to rise and uncover many things that are covered up.

There is a plan to try to silence the Prophetic Voice and prophecy. But the Lord said no one can stop His plans.
There are 6 popular churches (denominations) in Jamaica and the Lord says that if you don't take heed and change, then He will allow you to be exposed.

Within now and the next 12 months we will see a lot of signs and wonders that will take place globally. Miracles and knowledge upon His people will increase to carry out His Work.

There will be 6 event changes that will take place in the world.

A very powerful church will be coming under persecution. God will also raise up the children who will begin to preach, teach, prophesy and speak in tongues.

More disasters will break out globally. History will change its course only those who understand God's ways will understand His doings. But in it all there will be greater collaboration and great healing will take place.

# PROPHETIC WORD FOR MAY
# MOBILIZATION FOR YOUR INHERITANCE
(Numbers 1, 2 & 3)
By: Apostle Dr. Steve Lyston

The month of May – which is the second month of the traditional Jewish calendar - is critical to every believer. It is the most prophetic month for the year. It is the month of *Iyyar*, which means *Increase in Revelation*. So, May is the month of Revelation. It is a time of mobilization, when God is putting the family in order and battle array to march into the Promised Land. It is a time of record and evaluation to see who is ready to be on the Lord's side.

May is a time of selection. God is selecting His people for their purpose and their assignment, and He is pouring out. We will feel the Shekinah Glory like never before to lead us through Egypt. It is a time of healing and deliverance, renewal and strength.

Many things will begin to be rebuilt and re-established; God will deal with the Government of God/the Church, the Civil Government and the Family. God is shifting us from enslavement to occupation and dominion. It is a time of consecration, increase, the supernatural provision for the vision, fresh manna (Exodus 16)

It is a time of fresh revelation and instruction, redemption, and spiritual transformation and cleansing. (Leviticus 28: 15 – 16)

Anticipate great revelations.

Also, Isaiah 55: 12 – 14, it is a time when secret enemies will be revealed and exposed, particularly those within the Body of Christ. The Judases within the Body of Christ and the Political arena – particularly those advisors and counselors of government. Some are double agents and they will be found out.

1. This is the time the Absaloms and Ahithophels will meet their demise.

2. It is critical for leaders to examine those around them with serious pitfalls to watch out for betrayal.

3. This is the month that the Lord will bring conspiracies down to naught.

4. This is the month of double for your trouble.

5. Prodigals shall return and conspiracies, plots and generational curses shall be brought to naught.

6. God shall turn the counsel of the enemy to foolishness as in 2 Samuel 15: 31 which says, "Then someone told David, saying, "Ahithophel is among the conspirators with Absalom." And David said, "O Lord, I pray, turn the counsel of Ahithophel into foolishness!"

7. It is a month of proper recordkeeping and administration.

8. The faithful shall experience great spiritual, financial and material blessing as well as an increase in Spiritual gifts; and God shall lead us into a place of plenty.

9. Begin to dig ditches! (2 Kings 3: 16 - 17)

# THE PROPHETIC WORD OF THE LORD
## Signs of the Times Everywhere
By: Apostle Dr. Steve Lyston
June 24, 2018

Daniel 12: 4 says: *"But you, Daniel, shut up the words, and seal the book until the time of the end; many shall run to and fro, and knowledge shall increase."*

We are seeing the fulfillment of the Books of Daniel and Revelation right before our eyes. Revelation 13: 16 - 17 says: *"He causes all, both small and great, rich and poor, free and slave, to receive a mark on their right hand or on their foreheads, and that no one may buy or sell except one who has the mark or the name of the beast, or the number of his name."*

As we watch global news daily from politics to wars to immigration issues and the racial divide, the enemy has been using all this as a major distraction so that we don't pay attention to the laws being passed by different nations faster than we can blink. So many are not aware of what these laws are or even mean for each and all of us. We have seen major changes in the banking and remittance services. Most banks no longer take cash. These days we are faced with the decision of identifying ourselves through either voice or face recognition. So, passwords are becoming obsolete. Airports are utilizing those technologies also, particularly for the international flights. We are seeing rapid growth in the use of robots and other means of Artificial Intelligence or A.I. In fact, television commercials sensitizing every viewer on the uses and benefits of A.I. are shown daily.

Other countries are rapidly improving and increasing their identification systems. Organizations are rapidly linking departments together on the premise of security.

I believe very shortly, there will be chaos in the Social Security system.

Politically right now there is a very thin line dividing political parties and it is just a matter of who will advance the anti-Christ system more quickly. One party loves red skin potatoes and the other loves Idaho potatoes. At the end of the day a potato is a potato.

People who get benefits from the government will be at the greatest disadvantage. For them to get benefits, they will have to agree to be guinea pigs. Furthermore, everything will be focused on digital and cyber technology, and it will become commonplace in society and in our language.

Please recognize that the anti-Christ is not omnipresent or sovereign, hence only through the technological revolution can he control the minds of the people.

Today, your vehicle, house, appliances, security system, home entertainment systems, phones and hand-held devices are all connected and some of the laws that have been put in place dictate that you don't have to be told or to give permission for those behind the technology to access your information (public or private).

## Population Control

We are about to see the greatest move with regard to controlling the population nationally and globally, as many nations are now fearful of other nations becoming numerically and racially superior to theirs. So we will begin to see global immigration laws change to facilitate that. Even the denial of citizenship regardless of birth and dependent on the paternal citizenship. Border control systems, security fences, and electronic monitoring will be the order of the day; and hospitals, remittance services will be pressured. The poor will suffer and we will begin to see Genesis 11 again, when nations, leaders want to build a government without God.

God specifically spoke in Genesis 9 says "…"Be fruitful and multiply, and fill the earth." It has always been God's will and desire for man to travel throughout the earth freely, not to be restricted, limited or prevented from fulfilling His instructions.

While the choices politically will be poor, people will still need to make a choice.

Countries that try to advance certain anti-Christ laws upon the people before God's appointed time, their economies, particularly tourism, farming and travel industries, will crash.

No nation can build without God or try to advance any system before God's timing, and it is critical for advisors to begin advising leaders responsibly, recognizing that they are accountable from all angles. They must know Times and Seasons.

# THE PROPHETIC WORD OF THE LORD TO NATIONS
July 30, 2018

*The Word of the Lord through Apostle Steve Lyston, Bishop Doris Hutchinson and Prophetess Sophia DiMuccio*

1. The Lord says there is going to be a global shift in the political arena, in the Church, throughout the business sector and into nations. We are about to see a new wave of disasters, signs and wonders as we have never seen before, because the cries of the poor have come up before God. They are forsaken – the poor, the fatherless and the widow are forsaken and many have burned incense to false gods. God shall bring down their gods and idols.

2. There are many angels that have been released – many angels on horses riding into the following countries because of the covenant and agreements that they have signed. There is going to be an explosion and a removing of the covers.

   - United States of America
   - Jamaica
   - Russia
   - Japan
   - China
   - South Korea
   - Norway
   - India
   - Yemen

- Pakistan
- Britain
- Iraq
- Iran

3. Jamaica has been making agreements with other nations that engage in evil and they have been making arrangements which are displeasing to God in an effort to bring money into the country. No IMF money – so they are selling out the country through immorality and compromise to get more money into the country. Money received is being shared for their personal use on both sides. It is also being shared among some in the business community as well as some in the church fraternal. God shall expose. You will see many of the Churchmen beginning to drive classy cars because they are a part of the immoral agreement, and they will be using it to show their congregation that they are being blessed. This atmosphere of the false blessings is facilitated in many of the churches and will put a further strain on the people to support their lifestyle. 15 are spiritual advisors attached to both parties. It is through this that they are able to expand.

4. In Jamaica, there is too much pressure on the poor. While they are pressured to pay taxes, especially land taxes, most authorities within the nation don't pay taxes while the poor are under the strain to do so. The Lord says He will expose and remove the covering. Many of them will resign and leave the nation.

5. There is a major explosion that will take place between China and the USA. It has to do with a married diplomat and politicians who are raping and sexually abusing young boys and girls.

6. The next election in Jamaica is going to be very interesting. Anything can happen! Many will be storing away resources to flee from the nation.

# THE PROPHETIC WORD OF THE LORD FOR THE 3ᴿᴰ QUARTER
# August 2018

*Through Apostle Dr. Steve Lyston, Bishop Dr. Doris Hutchinson, and Prophetess Sophia DiMuccio*

1. There will be shaking, weeping, wailing, perplexity, remorse coming for those who reject God and His Word. Many will be confused and in awe. Many have blasphemed and it will be too late for them; and for them mercy is gone and judgement has come! God is calling everyone to go home and find a place or make an altar and cry out for what is coming upon the earth.

2. There is a great emerging of false prophets, there will be duplication of miracles and great deception and great infiltration will take place in the Church. The deception will be great in this end time. (2 Timothy 3: 8)

3. The entire world is about to experience great changes. Many lifestyles will change and be greatly disrupted in every aspect of life on earth. No more comfort zones.

4. Travelling to other countries will not solve the problem that will be impacting the globe.

5. Scientists will have great problems trying to understand the atmospheric conditions that will be affecting the earth.
6. All liquid substances that we consume we should pray over them before we ingest them. There are things put in them that are not good for our health all because of greed. The Lord says that we must take care of our bodies because incurable diseases are on the rise of which many are not aware.

7. Many are sick in their bodies and the doctors cannot find the complaint. When it is revealed, it will be too late. This condition is the result of sinful acts, and it will be difficult to find cures to deal with the problem.

8. Be careful of the animals you mingle with – even pets.

9. A time is coming where no country will be able to help the other – because of the vast number of disasters that will be taking place.

10. There will be great problems with the communication systems. Massive disruption with land and water worldwide. Major attacks will take place on communication systems.

11. The Lord is about to visit the Oval Office. Many Democrats and Republicans will be exposed for maliciousness, deception.

12. More fires will take place within the USA,

because the treatment and the cry of the poor treatment have gone up to the Lord.

13. God is about to call home soon, some of those who refuse to listen to His Word, especially some world leaders.

14. We cannot fix our country with sinful actions, they will only bring the wrath and disasters at the hand of God. (John 5: 29)

**Jamaica**

15. The Lord says He is ready to visit Jamaican and every man must prepare for His visitation. There is too much fighting in and falling apart of the family. Your children are going astray. Some have left home and are fearful of returning. Some are dead while some are in dangerous company. Many parents have sleepless nights because of their children. The Lord says begin to speak the word of God over their lives and you will begin to see change. The Lord says that many have rejected God's word spoken by His prophets and because they are not taking heed, many will be cut off without remedy. (Luke 13: 1 – 5)

16. Warning to all Christian Leaders - live holy lives

(1 Corinthians 9: 27)

17. Christians will be tested greatly. Seek God in prayer and fasting. Remember God is loving and forgiving and ready to save the lost.

18. Jamaica will burn like Sodom. Prepare for a great drought as has never been seen before. All high rising buildings in Jamaica will be shaken. Some will fall to the ground. Water will also break out of places where there is no water.

19. Go home and remove the idols that you have hidden and have been worshipping as gods, or after a while, they will have you to do unspeakable things against God's will.

20. Payback the large sums of money you owe. You know who you are. **Warning**: A trap is set for you.

21. Government! Things are travelling under the sea of which you are unaware. Open your eyes.

22. Leaders of the nation and Members of Parliament – display proper examples for the young ones to follow! You are all accountable unto God and He will remove you. Go's eyes are watching you.

23. There is more exposure and more deception and disappointment coming. No one must point fingers. How many of you are free from corruption?

24. A massive financial scandal is about to be exposed. There is infiltration in the army. The evil deeds you are planning will come back at you and your family and will cause shame and disgrace to them. Be warned! The time of exposure is now. Secret deals have been made that should have been made known to the country, but it was hidden and it will come out. Both secular society and Christendom, be warned! God is angry with your evil deeds! Be warned!

## The Body of Christ

25. Shifting, Shaking and Sifting is about to take place! God is visiting all Churches,

26. The Lord is about to uproot anything planted which is not of Him, including doctrines and systems.

27. We are about to see a refocusing on Christ as the Center of the Church again; and He will bring His people back to a lifestyle of truth. There is

going to be an emergence of deliverance ministries which will set the captives free.

28. As God shakes the political systems, there is coming a time when the Church will be called upon to assist in the governance of the nation to prevent total collapse. The eyes of many will open because God is raising up the Ezekiel 34 "Good Shepherds "to gather and feed His people.
29. There is going to be a war against the altar of Satan – against witchcraft, against sexual immorality and against the attacks on the family. He wants His people to read the book of Ephesians.

30. God is calling His people to make a greater effort in feeding the poor and the less fortunate.

31. There will be a coming together – a remnant – who will put the Kingdom's business first not there denomination.

32. There will be more Five-fold ministries that God will raise up as He is continuing to shake down the Old Order. Holiness will be preached again without compromise.

33. We are about to see the zeal return to the local

Church and revival within Europe, Latin Nations and the Caribbean.

34. The enemy will try to pass new laws in an effort to block new churches from being planted. Some of the opposition will come from those who are in the Fivefold that have become religious.

# VORTEX EMERGING!
By: Apostle Dr. Steve Lyston
August 28, 2018

On Saturday, August 26, 2017 the Lord spoke and said that the globe and the Church should study and prepare for the Vortex! A Vortex is "a mass of fluid (such as a liquid) with a whirling or circular motion that tends to form a cavity or vacuum in the center of the circle and to draw toward this cavity or vacuum bodies subject to its action; (especially whirlpool/tornado/whirlwind, cyclone, black-hole, swirl and so on).

There are many instances spiritually where scripture mentions the whirlwind which is in fact a kind of vortex.

Jeremiah 25: 32 says, "Thus says the Lord of hosts: "Behold, disaster shall go forth From nation to nation, and a great whirlwind shall be raised up from the farthest parts of the earth."

Jeremiah 30: 23 also says, "Behold, the whirlwind of the Lord Goes forth with fury, a continuing whirlwind; it will fall violently on the head of the wicked" and,

Ezekiel 1: 4 tells us "Then I looked, and behold, a whirlwind was coming out of the north, a great cloud with raging fire engulfing itself; and brightness was all around it and radiating out of its midst like the color of amber, out of the midst of the fire."

There are many other instances even in 2 Kings 2, where we see that suddenly a chariot of fire came and the Prophet Elijah was caught up in a whirlwind which signifies many things including:

- A generational shift
- The emerging of the Elijah company
- Spiritual and Physical Promotion
- Transfer of Mantles and
- Wealth Transfer to the faithful generation

Job 37: 9 says: "From the chamber of the south comes the whirlwind, and cold from the scattering winds of the north."

We need to look at 2 things:

- Continents within the North and South
- States within the north and south in the USA

## Continents

### North

North America
Canada
Upper Africa
Europe
Asia

### South

South America
Lower Africa
Australia
Antarctica

Interestingly the ice is melting rapidly in Antarctica which means water levels are rising.

The following are those states in the USA that are deemed to be the Northern and Southern States according to Britannica.com which cites this as the basis on which the states are referred to as Northern and Southern States.

*"The North, region, northern United States, historically identified as the free states that opposed slavery and the Confederacy during the American Civil War."*

| **North** | **South** |
|---|---|
| North Dakota | West Virginia |
| South Dakota | Maryland |
| Nebraska | Texas |
| Minnesota | Delaware |
| Iowa | Virginia |
| Wisconsin | Florida |
| Indiana | Kentucky |
| Michigan | Oklahoma |
| Ohio | Arkansas |
| Pennsylvania | Louisiana |
| New York | Mississippi |
| Vermont | Alabama |
| New Hampshire | Tennessee |
| Massachusetts | Georgia |
| Connecticut | North Carolina |
| Rhode Island | South Carolina |
| Maine | |
| New Jersey | |

Kansas
Missouri
Illinois

The Vortex is the reason there is such a divide right now within the United States because many unresolved and deep-seated issues still remain and they are resurfacing now because God is going to deal with it. But we have to know that it can only be dealt with spiritually.

So, we are going to see similar significant stirrings in the political, civil, business, religious, spiritual, and financial arenas. We have to pray for an awakening and a revival because that is the only way healing can take place.

**The Vortex in the Justice System**

Job 38:1
Job 40: 6
Psalm 58: 8 – 10

There will be a cleansing in the Justice System, particularly among judges. Justice is symbolically pictured as a balance of scales weighing Justice impartially to bring peace. However, the earthly judges have repeatedly tipped the scales to cause or insight violence, and now the Chief Judge – the Most High of the Highest Supreme Court is about to hold earthly judges accountable for their actions in the justice system.

# The Vortex in the Business and Financial Sectors

Psalm 77: 18 – 20
Proverbs 1: 27
Proverbs 10: 25
Isaiah 21: 1
Isaiah 17: 1 – 4
Isaiah 40: 23 - 24

There will be a shaking in business – distress and anguish. Creditors and international lenders, the Tax Department, Communications, Pharmaceuticals, Banks and Healthcare will experience great shaking so that the poor will be able to rise.

There will be judgement on the Gaming Control Board and some lobby groups as well as those Non-profit that say they are there to help the poor but are simply extracting from both ends of the spectrum for themselves.

The kind of shaking that is coming, no man will be able to have control over what will be going on. No one can stop it.

# The Atmospheric Vortex

We will continue to see flooding and other disasters occurring. But while it may be disaster for some it will be great blessings for others and opportunities will be created. Sometimes, jobs are created, new sources of energy found, inventions are realized in the midst of the greatest disasters.

We have seen many of the poor experience foreclosure on their homes. They were never given a chance to save their homes. The vortex that is emerging will bring a switch where the rich will be the ones losing their properties. It will be blessing for the poor and judgement on the unjust. This will also bring many back to the Lord and bring many nations to Him.

**Vortex in the Body of Christ**

A whirlwind will blow which will separate the false from the true – a purging of the hirelings, wolves, false teachers, false shepherds, money changers and merchandizers from the Church; and a moving out of those who pull people to themselves rather than leading them to Christ and Truth to prepare His people for the rapture. This vortex will also cause many to see the supernatural unfold. For example, a vortex transported Philip from one place to the other. Acts 8: 39 – 40 says, "Now when they came up out of the water, the Spirit of the Lord caught Philip away, so that the eunuch saw him no more; and he went on his way rejoicing. But Philip was found at Azotus. And passing through, he preached in all the cities till he came to Caesarea."

See also:

- 1 Kings 18: 12
- 2 Kings 2: 11 – 12
- John 6: 21

- Genesis 5: 24

Furthermore, among the true ones, there will be promotion at and to all levels and of all kinds.

God is the one allowing the stir through the vortex to bring out His will and purpose. Things that were buried will be uprooted and exposed.
While the enemy can cause a vortex also, as we see in the book of Exodus between Moses and Pharaoh, let us rise up as servants of God, that God's true will and purpose will be accomplished in the earth, so that hearts will be changed and souls will be saved. Leaders – religious and political will walk in proper alignment so that communities will be transformed and there will be equality in distribution of resources, and in the education system to allow opportunities for ALL. The leaders will have Godly motives not their motives.

# THE WORD OF THE LORD
September 10, 2018

*Bishop Dr. Doris Hutchinson and Prophetess Sophia DiMuccio*

1. More disasters will be taking place. Sand will be piling up in some parts of the world and this will cause water to be directed to different places which did not have water before, as a sign.

2. We should pray for the small islands in the Caribbean – Turks & Caicos, The Cayman Islands, The Bahamas, and all the other small islands in the Caribbean as well as Jamaica. Pray against those islands disappearing under the sea as a result of disasters.

3. Pray for Louisiana especially New Orleans.

4. Pray, because more disasters will be taking place in India, New Jersey, Boston, Kentucky, and The Carolinas.

5. Those with massive investments in the agricultural industry will suffer great losses as a result of the disasters and it will cause a massive shortage in food including, peanuts, potatoes and other vegetables. This will cause a major famine throughout the world. But, the Lord says, "If My people who are called by my name will cry out, then I will show mercy, and My people will be fed during the famine. As they

obey Me, worship Me and give their Tithe, they will be protected."

6. Pray for all places where oil is found and all places where the drilling is taking place, as there will be many disasters. Most of them will crash and workers will be running frantically. It will cause an oil shortage and increase the prices significantly.

7. God is reminding the rich that He is God.

**Leadership**

8. Political leaders must stop bickering and fighting against each other. They need to be united and come together to deal with what is coming globally. Many of them have turned their backs on the poor. No one should be penalized because of the party they support when it comes to the distribution of resources. That is what has led to the increase in poverty. Unless leaders repent, God says He will drive them like animals out of their positions.

9. God is the only one that can fix what is broken down. Politicians need to begin to bow down to Him, seek Him for divine direction and stop undermining each other or else God will replace them. When Jonathon attacked and defeated the Philistines, it was because of God acting on his behalf to grant him help. There are going to be drastic changes coming up on the globe. Also, there will be a season of newness.

10. The entire universe is not lacking in God's Word, so many will not have an excuse when the shaking comes.

11. God places leaders in position to help other human beings and utilizes all that lies in their power. But too many hidden motives and desires have caused many to suffer. The Lord says His hand shall be heavy upon them.

12. There are some countries that are seeking God secretly for help, but God will send help for them.

13. Too many are double-minded and too many are living a double-standard life. Many leaders in the Body of Christ are doing things – gossiping and slandering each other. God will expose them unless they repent. In the Body of Christ, we are in a continuous season of preparation, so there must be change in one's lifestyle.

## Jamaica

14. In the next general election in Jamaica there will be many surprises.

15. Politicians must live a clean life and not engage in hiring anyone to take another's life. The poor are suffering while they lie to the people. They must remember that they have mothers, sisters and brothers.

16. What is the purpose of getting into politics if you are not there to help the people? Is it to enjoy the perks? Politicians must do what is right because they will have to stand before God and give an account. Is your soul right before God? They must remember King David. He humbled himself and repented before God. The lifestyle of each politician will affect the people. The sin of David caused conspiracy, treason and brought plagues upon the nation. Many are plotting and pulling away the wealth from the lives of the people. For the Lord says, "I have seen your lifestyle, and a time of judgement is coming."

# THE PROPHETIC WORD OF THE LORD
November 12, 2018
Amos 9

The Lord is going to have the Praise and Worship that He deserves, and He will restore what has fallen so that His praises come from the heart of His people. "The time of division is at hand. I shall separate My people which are called by My name. They shall rejoice and be blessed. Many that have lost My love, through My faithful ones they will be restored."

1. The Lord is about to go through churches. Those who are not living according to His will and in obedience will be separated.

2. Mighty ones displaced and their glory taken away because they refuse to serve and obey Me in Spirit and in Truth. The homes of the unfaithful will be desolate. They will persecute those who are living (right). I am about to do a thing in the land. Hearts will fail – ears will tingle for then shall the people know that I Am the I Am. I have been warning the rebellious nations through My servants I have chosen carry. You shall live to see My words come to pass and many shall bow before Me and repent.

3. I have been in the media worldwide no one will have another chance. I will anoint My chosen ones, outpouring of My Spirit upon you which will bring knowledge. I shall increase your knowledge. I shall reveal many things that will marvel you! Be strong

My servants. God forth with My banner and many shall fall down before Me and worship Me in Spirit and in Truth.

4. A worldwide event will take place. Be courageous my son and daughter. Let no one deter you. I have called you and positioned you. I have seen your affliction – only for a while – your victory and deliverance are coming. I have hidden you in my pavilion.

5. There are places where your words must get to. Carry on, I am leading you.

6. There are countries that your words and teaching must reach. And it shall come to pass. Leaders – men and women – for I will reveal their deeds through My words that shall be spoken and written.

7. A set of Chinese that need to hear my words, they shall hear it for they have been deceived. Their deliverance is (at hand).

8. There is controversy in Jamaica's politics between the two leaders. Hidden things are there to be exposed. For Jamaica to be delivered, their eyes must be opened. There are those being led into the secret worship of idols. Deliverance is coming for them. I will send help to deliver My people.

9. Mighty angels are watching over My faithful. Great disasters could displace Jamaica, but I love them, and (I will protect them.)

10. And if the great world leaders will not adhere to My words and obey them. I will remove them and show them a sign. I will reveal their hearts to themselves.

11. Many have subtly robbed ... But I am! For the poor – in heart and substance – I will be their God and provide.

12. There is going to be a change.

13. Servants, cease not to pray for Jamaica, for I have loved them.

14. A great disruption of the earth has begun, for my words shall not return to me void but shall accomplish what it was sent to do. (Isaiah 55: 10 – 11)

15. The deception is leaders have spoken one thing and do the opposite and corruption for my people.

16. Swords are wielding. Those swords are going to cleanse the land, because they mocked my words which are life. Many are building private places to hide, but they cannot hide.

17. Great surprises shall come from the North, South, East and West – worldwide.

18. Great provision is made for My people as they humble themselves.

19. Britain is in trouble. America is following.

20. Even Russia is rising but will not last for long.

21. A great undermining is coming! The leaders of other countries infiltrating other countries they think have oil and other resources to rob them of it. It is worldwide.

22. There are scientists trained to go into countries as tourists and learn everything from the locals. They have been sent. But it shall come to pass that a worldwide, evangelistic encounter will hit the earth and the Holy Ghost will be with My people and there are those who will bow.

23. "Anointed men and women will be travelling to and fro to hear My words." Here comes the end~

**Jamaica**

24. Our security men are not trustworthy – the army

and the police force – and thy will do anything to be rich.

25. Watch (Paul) Robertson (St. Thomas)

26. Watch (Douglas) Vaz
27. What Apostle Steve Speaks on the TBC is convicting those religious men and they want him to stop. It disturbs them. These broadcasts will be rolling on the screens of heaven, and we will be seeing our deeds there. These broadcasts were to help them desist from their wrongs. They are helping people. The people are listening, and they are learning.

28. Jamaica is going down.

29. Andrew Holness should take a stand against abortion. If Jamaica endorses abortion it will go down.

30. God is going to move some leaders – public, private and religious. They no longer consult God. When they come together in the House, those who know better should call prayer. They (Parliament) should call true men and women of God to pray.

31. Open Vision: A parish where water is spewing out and no man knows the origin.

32. Some of the things the leader are coming out

33. against and opposing – they are the same ones who secretly started or supported it. They claim the economy is growing, but God says it is growing for a FALL!

34. Legalizing marijuana would be the worst thing they could ever do. Everyone will be negatively affected by it. They want to make millions, but many will not have use to themselves. They need to go back to the drawing board. How are they going to control it when they legalize marijuana?

35. Watch Peter Phillips, Phillip Paulwell, Mark Golding, Lisa Hanna

36. There is serious undermining taking place in the JLP

37. Drastic measures will have to be taken in the Army and Police Force.

38. Andrew Holness operates with a double tongue.

39. The police and the army have become corrupt.

40. They bring in their friends to do what they want.

If they continue, people will lose confidence in them, and they will ask for a new army and police force. (Recruiting and Promoting, greed is the reason) Don't be surprised if they take down a politician.

41. A scandal will break in Jamaica where every man is going to hold down his head and be ashamed of being Jamaican.

42. There are organizations in Jamaica that could help people and make the nation better, but the heads of the nation conspire to keep certain people down.

43. Don't trust GUY

44. Peter Phillips and Miguel Phillips – watch him and pray for them.

45. Pray for Pearnell Charles and Pearnell Charles Jr.

46. Audly Shaw can't get along with Andrew Holness.

47. "DON'T FIGHT, HOLINESS! Don't come against holiness."

48. There are no more secrets in our nation (Jamaica). It has been infiltrated and resources are being taken from our land and sea.

49. Our very water is in danger. We are losing our quality water.

50. There are Trojan horses in our midst.

51. The Lord says He is going to shake Parliament and shake some of them out. What they should do for the nation they are not doing it. There is partiality with favors to friends but God is going to expose it all. They know the right thing to do but because of position and politics they do the wrong. They think they are untouchable.

52. Both sides have upcoming plans whoever wins the nation doesn't know about. Some of the laborites and PNP are close friends. They go behind people's backs and make plans. When they come into power they continue the sin.

53. There are serious deceptions ahead. But the world of God is reaching them and if they don't come out and repent, God is going to deal with them.

54. or Watch P J Patterson. He needs to repent now else! He is going to be held accountable for many things. He is still working undercover.

55. A time is coming when the gospel will not be

preached as freely as it is now in Jamaica, as many want to change the Scriptures to suit their lifestyle and change the way they teach religious education in Jamaica. If they continue to change the word to fit their lifestyle He will visit them. Be warned Jamaica! God will visit the nation.

56. Pray for the Martha Brae River and that entire area. Pray for exposure.

57. Pray for Kingston Wharves and the Norman Manley International Airport. Pray against corruption and that things will not tarnish the nation. Pray also that disaster will not hit Kingston Wharves. Pray against an increase in contract killings.

# THE PROPHETIC WORD OF THE LORD
## December 1, 2018

1. Bishops and Pastors do not enter into any (spiritually) unlawful covenants.

2. More journalists will be murdered as they try to expose high level corruption.

3. Many birds will be falling from the sky in Poland

4. Millions of fish will continue to die on a global level and contamination will increase.

5. If businesses and investors will not seek God for guidance regarding business and investing and understanding the times and season many will be blown out of the water. Many CEOs will lose their jobs as a result of lack of solutions.

6. Pray for TBN as trouble looms.

7. Pray for Jamaica to stop divestment before it is too late because that will negatively impact on the nation's economy and its future.

8. We will see the manifestation of Revelation 13 and Revelation 17 in the earth.

9. Unless the leadership styles of many leaders global change, and unless they seek God and listen to the

people, many will be swept out of office and lose power.

10. God is calling on the Kingdom people to begin to do the things He has instructed them quickly as the Kingdom of Heaven is at hand.

11. Watch March 2019. Many things will happen. There will be shakings. Many will ask why, others will say "it can't be!" We will also see in some parts of the earth, drought like never before.

12. 2019 is the Year of the Church. There will be many stirrings and shakings, because judgement must begin in the House of the Lord first.

13. 2019 we will see exposure at levels we have never seen before, particularly among political leaders globally. There will be many plots, fabrications, murders and the question many will ask is "Who can we trust?" Many who are speaking against corruption are the ones who are actually involved. The Lord says no one is safe – He will expose.

14. As nations continue to digitize, we will see more fraud, more hacking, more cyber-crimes and more trouble than we bargained for.

15. There is a plan to undermine Jamaica and tarnish her image internationally because certain mandates and motives regarding gender, abortion and the removal of the patriarchal references are not moving at the speed that was anticipated or expected. Jamaica Tourist Board needs to be careful of the alliances and covenants that they would engage in, in an effort to grow tourism, as it will backfire, and a scandal will break out on the country. Be warned! They need to seek God for the marketing strategies and solutions.

# 2019: CHANGE WITHIN WILL BRING POSITIVE CHANGE
By: Apostle Steve Lyston
Received December 28, 2018

Everybody is crying out for change and are debating what kind of change they want to see. Some are talk of political change, others talk about change in the marketplace, some talk about individual changes in their lives – new personal resolutions and goals; still others talk about climate change – all kinds of changes. Over the past 10 years we have seen a lot of changes taking place, but most of them are negative. What was once considered despicable has now become "honorable". The poor are forgotten more and more as the years go by as compassion and care lessen with time. The global priorities have been turned upside down and we are heading down a dangerous path; even those coming on the scene talking of change come mainly with deception. The only truly positive changes that have remained and will continue to remain truly positive are the positive changes that take place of heart, mind and lifestyle. Further to that, our motives, the way we think and how we function on a daily basis affects even our very environment. So that, regardless of how much we say about climate change, we will only see the climate change we are looking for when man begins to change. If we keep doing the same negative thing, how do we get positive change?

Regardless of what plans, goals and objectives we have – personal, national or global – if our lifestyle, mindset and heart remain the same, we will not get the positive results we are seeking.

## Change Fosters Change

Oftentimes we hear people complain that politicians are not doing anything and that they want better. But how will they get better if they themselves remain the same – having the same heart, same mind, the same lifestyle? They don't attract better because they choose to remain the same. Likewise, people say they want a society without God, so why do they complain when crime, violence and shooting takes place? Some say they want a better security force, but continue to maintain low wages for security personnel and neglect the people? The society we create is the society will get. When we build from the blueprint of other nations or with the plans of others, then we will face what they face and get their "plagues" in addition to our own internal issues. We don't need another wall, we don't need bigger walls, we don't need more prisons, we don't need Biometric systems, we don't need RFIDs – we need a heart, mind and lifestyle change. Implementing system without God does not stop corruption – all we are doing is passing the plate of corruption to different hands. So we embrace the same system being passed on to friends and opportunists to continue sharing from the same plate of corruption and no true and positive change happens.

Oftentimes people create "new" systems to deal with the problems, but all they are doing is neglecting the real issue to be dealt with and ignoring the real solutions. What happens when a person who is broke and in debt, continues to do nothing to change it while expecting the change? They will remain in debt while the situation worsens. There are even pastors who want their church to change but remain with the same mindset and the same way of doing business. So they can make all the declarations they want to make, if they don't change their mindset and how they do things, everything will remain the same.

**Self-Evaluation**

Every person now has to evaluate him/herself. Everyone must remember that however we treat others, so shall we be treated – what you sow you will reap. We don't believe in karma, we believe in retribution and seedtime and harvest.

Many people have used the power, grace and favor that God has given to them to negatively impact the lives of others. Many are on the street now without food. Some will say it was a business decision. Are you willing to hear those same words said to you in the year ahead? What are you willing to change as you come to the close of the year in order to see a positive change in the year ahead? You have the answer.

# 2019

# THE WORD OF THE LORD FOR THE NATIONS 2019 AND ONWARD

*Through Prophetess Doris Hutchinson, Apostle Steve Lyston, Prophetess Michelle Lyston, Prophetess Sophia DiMuccio, Prophetess Nadra Brotherton and Prophet O. Onesto Jolly.*

The year 2019 / 5779 – is the Year of the Church. There will be many stirrings and shakings, because judgement must begin in the House of the Lord first. A lot of shaking and shifting will take place in the earth also. God is calling His people to win the harvest at any cost. There is going to be a time a double portion, restoration, and restitution, for those that have been faithful and those that have loss. There will be purging, purifying, and mass healing will pour out in the earth for those have been afflicted. God says as we lift Him up, He will bring great men unto us. Many curses shall be broken and many tongues will be silent in 2019. We will also see the manifestation of Haggai 1:11. There will be drought upon the Land/Ground, Mountain, Grain, New Wine, Oil, Men, Livestock and the Labor of Your Hands. Also, in 2019/5779, we will see A New Era New Cycles, New Direction, New Counsel, Now Faith (The Manifestation), God's Supernatural Power, Wisdom, Intercessory Prayer, and Increase Of Grace

The Anti-Christ spirit will rise as never before. Many countries will begin to release Radio-frequency identification (RFID), biometrics, and tracking devices, especially within the poor. Many will come in ID forms and other formats. (Revelation 13) As in Revelations 13, the Beast, and the dragon will blaspheme God and ridicule

Christians. A system is coming in place in the West and will be revealed in America that will open the eyes of Christians in America. It has already started in Canada and Europe.

There will be great problems with the communication systems. Massive disruption with land and water worldwide. Major attacks will take place on communication systems.

Many storms will come to an end and they will begin to receive the goodness of God upon their life. Also a lot of birthing will take place in 2019. A lot of people will be getting pregnant, spiritual and natural conception will take place in 2019. It will also be the Year of the Rainbow, dealing with universal covenant, and righteousness. A lot of false doctrines will arise and many will be deceived in 2019. It will also be the year of blessing and curse (Genesis 9: 25 – 29). The year of agreement, covenant, circumcision, and consecration. We will see a lot of agreements and circumcisions. Abraham was 99 years of age and circumcised physically. (Genesis 17: 24)

2019/5779 is the year of Restoration, the Holy Spirit, Jubilee, and Liberty. (Leviticus 25:10) Universality, the year of the 9 fruits of the Spirit. The year of Harvest, Fruit of your labor, and also we see the manifestation of the 9 gifts of the spirit. (Galatians 5:22-23; 1 Corinthians 12:8-10)

2019/5779, the year of Atonement, Preparation, Obedience, **Intercession**, Redemption, blessing from above for the faithful. The year of Jesus Christ and His blood.

(Leviticus 9) Grace and finality, judgement, and divine completeness. Righteous ordinance. Many will be set free form the wilderness, oppression, and bondage; and then they cross over in 2019. It will also be the year of confusion and the tower of Babel will fall. There will be manifestation of evil spirit that will manifest in humans that has never seen before. Additionally, 2019 is a year of great deception and God is calling the Body of Christ to cry out for Discernment of Spirits. Be careful who you endorse and what you endorse. If a person's focus is not on Jesus Christ, then they will fall away. (Jeremiah 17: 5 – 8).

Watch March 2019. Many things will happen. There will be shakings. Many will ask why, others will say "it can't be!" We will also see in some parts of the earth, drought like never before. Massive starvation will take place that even the very rich will be impacted. The playing field will be leveled. For the Lord said he will make provision for the poor who have been despised. Many poor shall begin to rise, more bush fire will break out in other areas and more lives will loss. The luxurious living for many rich will come to an end.

2019 we will see exposure at levels we have never seen before, particularly among political leaders globally. There will be many plots, fabrications, murders and the question many will ask is "Who can we trust?" Many who are speaking against corruption are the ones who are actually involved. The Lord says no one is safe – He will expose. More journalists will be murdered as they try to expose high level corruption.

There will be great deception that will hit both Christendom and the Secular. Many of the people will turn against their leader which will result in secret/contract killings. We will see economies rise in some countries and fall in others. There will be confusion and unknown illnesses. We will even see situations similar to the French Revolution of 1789 emerging once again.

A undermining is coming! The leaders of other countries infiltrating other countries they think have oil and other resources to rob them of it. It is worldwide. There are scientists trained to go into countries as tourists and learn everything from the locals. They have been sent. But it shall come to pass that a worldwide, evangelistic encounter will hit the earth and the Holy Ghost will be with My people and there are those who will bow.

Finally, 2019/5779 will also be the year of the manifestation of the 4 horses as in Revelation and Zechariah – the White Horse, Red Horse, Black Horse and the Pale Horse.

**White horse** - symbol of international power and politics. In the form of military conquest and global deception. Many countries will be conquered through loans that they are borrowing from other countries. Warning for countries that keep borrowing loans. Many loans will be default and many countries will find themselves in trouble.

**Red Horse** - Symbol of civil war and strife.

**Black Horse** - Symbol of economic disruption. Inflation, things will become scarce or shortage. Labor problems - low wages. Rampant starvation, and God wants them to stockpile. Stockpile water and gold. Great Shifts In The Global Economy!

**Pale Horse** - Symbol of disease and death, devastation that will break out. Shortage of medication that will take place. More problems within the ocean. More fish will die.

Study Revelation, read the seven letters to the church.

**The Word For Jamaica**

1. Servants, cease not to pray for Jamaica, for I have loved them. The Lord says He is ready to visit Jamaican and every man must prepare for His visitation. There is too much fighting in and falling apart of the family. Your children are going astray. Some have left home and are fearful of returning. Some are dead while some are in dangerous company. Many parents have sleepless nights because of their children. The Lord says begin to speak the word of God over their lives and you will begin to see change. The Lord says that many have rejected God's word spoken by His prophets and because they are not taking heed, many will be cut off without remedy. (Luke 13: 1 – 5)

2. There are 6 popular churches (denominations) in Jamaica and the Lord says that if you don't take heed and change, then He will allow you to be exposed.

3. Jamaica will burn like Sodom. Prepare for a great drought as has never been seen before. All high rising buildings in Jamaica will be shaken. Some will fall to the ground. Water will also break out of places where there is no water unless they repent.
4. There is controversy in Jamaica's politics between the two parties. Hidden things are there to be exposed. For Jamaica to be delivered, their eyes must be opened. There are those being led into the secret worship of idols. "Deliverance is coming, I will send help to deliver My people." (the Lord says.) There is a push to call early election in Jamaica, and if that is done, there will be riots and chaos. This is also connected to the killings taking place in the country.

5. The crime in Jamaica is well orchestrated with a greater motive behind it. If it is successful in achieve its goals then there will be a switch and it will be too late by the time the people of Jamaica's eyes open, it will be too late. There needs to be closer monitoring of all airlines coming into the country – publicly or privately. The airports need to tighten up their security at the airports.

6. Great exposure will take place in the financial sector. It is about land and other resources. The global and local media will begin to rise and uncover many things that are covered up. A massive financial scandal is about to be exposed. "The evil deeds you are planning will come back at you and your family and will cause shame and disgrace to them. Be

warned! The time of exposure is now. Secret deals have been made that should have been made known to the country, but it was hidden and it will come out. Both secular society and Christendom, be warned!" (says the Lord). God is angry with your evil deeds! Be warned!

7. There is a plan to undermine Jamaica and tarnish her image internationally because certain mandates and motives regarding gender, abortion and the removal of the patriarchal references are not moving at the speed that was anticipated or expected. Jamaica Tourist Board needs to be careful of the alliances and covenants that they would engage in, in an effort to grow tourism, as it will backfire, and a scandal will break out on the country. Be warned! They need to seek God for the marketing strategies and solutions.

8. Mighty angels are watching over My faithful. Great disasters could displace Jamaica, but I love them, and (I will protect them.) (There was an open vision of a parish where water is spewing out and no man knows the origin.)

9. Jamaica is going down the wrong path. The Prime Minister needs to take a stand against abortion. If Jamaica endorses abortion it will go down. Also, the gambling – lottery, betting, etc.) are bringing many into poverty and bankruptcy and is destroying families – especially the children and increases crime. The Government must now take a stand before it is too late.

10. God is going to move some leaders – public, private, political and religious. They no longer consult God. When they come together in the House, those who know better should call prayer. They (Parliament) should call true men and women of God to pray.

11. Some of the things the leader are coming out against and opposing – they are the same ones who secretly started or supported it. They claim the economy is growing, but God says it is growing for a FALL!

12. Legalizing marijuana would be the worst thing they could ever do. Everyone will be negatively affected by it. They want to make millions, but many will not have use to themselves. They need to go back to the drawing board. There will be little control. The Prime Minister needs to take a stand.

13. The army has been infiltrated and is becoming corrupt. They bring in their friends to do what they want. If they continue, people will lose confidence in them, and they will ask for a new army. (Recruiting and Promoting, greed is the reason). Drastic measures will have to be taken in the Army and Police Force.

14. Our security men are not trustworthy – the army

and the police force – and thy will do anything to be rich. The Spirit of the Lord says the police and soldiers need to be united to win the battles, and this is not the time for them to allow the spirit of pride to take control of them because many of the citizens will be hurt.

15. A scandal will break in Jamaica where every man is going to hold down his head and be ashamed of being Jamaican.

16. Pray for a popular, veteran, Jamaican morning radio personality, and for his health and salvation now before it is too late.

17. There are organizations in Jamaica that could help the people and make the nation better, but the heads of many organizations conspire to keep down certain people within the nation who can make the nation better, but the Lord shall move those corrupt ones.

18. There is serious undermining taking place in the JLP. Don't be surprised if they take down a politician.

19. What is the purpose of getting into politics if you are not there to help the people? Is it to enjoy the perks? Politicians must do what is right because they will have to stand before God and give an account. Is your soul right before God? They must remember King David. He

humbled himself and repented before God. The lifestyle of each politician will affect the people. The sin of David caused conspiracy, treason and brought plagues upon the nation. Many are plotting and pulling away the wealth from the lives of the people. For the Lord says, "I have seen your lifestyle, and a time of judgement is coming."

20. The Lord says pray for the following politicians Peter Phillips, Miguel Phillips, Pearnel Charles, Pearnel Charles Jr., Christopher Tufton, Audley Shaw, Andrew Holness, Phillip Paulwell, Mark Golding, Lisa Hanna, P. J. Patterson, Paul Robertson, Douglas Vaz – it is testing time. Pray also for their salvation; and pray for the healing of Dr. Kenneth Baugh.

21. Jamaica has been making agreements with other nations that engage in evil and they have been making arrangements which are displeasing to God in an effort to bring money into the country. There is stringency with the IMF, so they are selling out the country through immorality and compromise to get more money into the country. Money received is being shared for their personal use on both sides. It is also being shared among some in the business community as well as some in the church fraternal. God shall expose. You will see many of the Churchmen beginning to drive

classy cars because they are a part of the immoral agreement, and they will be using it to show their congregation that they are being blessed. This atmosphere of the false blessings is facilitated in many of the churches and will put a further strain on the people to support their lifestyle. 15 of them are spiritual advisors attached to both parties. It is through this that they are able to expand.

22. In Jamaica, there is too much pressure on the poor. While they are pressured to pay taxes, especially land taxes, most authorities within the nation don't pay taxes while the poor are under the strain to do so. The Lord says He will expose and remove the covering. Many of them will resign and leave the nation.

23. There are no more secrets in our nation (Jamaica). It has been infiltrated and resources are being taken from our land and sea. There are Trojan horses in our midst. Even our very water is in danger. We are losing our quality water.

24. The Lord says He is going to shake Parliament and shake some of them out. What they should do for the nation they are not doing it. There is partiality with favors to friends but God is going to expose it all. They know the right thing to do but because of position and politics they do the wrong. They think they are untouchable. There will be chaos and

confusion, they will be the order of the day within the political arena of Jamaica.

25. Both sides have upcoming plans whoever wins the nation doesn't know about. Some of the laborites and PNP are close friends. They go behind people's backs and make plans. When they come into power they will continue with their plans. There are serious deceptions ahead. But the word of God is reaching them and if they don't come out and repent, God is going to deal with them.

26. The Spirit of the Lord is exposing every Politician because their motives have been to deceive the citizens to get their votes. But, the Eyes of the Lord move to and fro throughout the earth and they have been weighed in the balances and found wanting. Daniel 5:27 (TEKEL) There is a great shift that is coming to Jamaican Politics, whereby the majority of votes will be awarded to fresh faces [young politicians] and more access will be given to certain genders. There are some Politicians who behave like extortionists because they are the ones pushing most of the crime, but the Spirit of the Lord says "Who unto those who do these things!"

27. The Lord says the Politicians need to genuinely

help the citizens of the Nation within each of their communities served. There are high-powered weapons that are being distributed within different communities as bribing to get their votes (ensuring that their votes are secured for the next election). In the next general election in Jamaica there will be many surprises.

28. A time is coming when the gospel will not be preached as freely as it is now in Jamaica, as many want to change the Scriptures to suit their lifestyle and change the way they teach religious education in Jamaica. If they continue to change the word to fit their lifestyle, He will visit them. Be warned Jamaica! God will visit the nation.

29. Pray for the Jamaican Dollar to maintain its value. Pray against manipulation and undermining of the dollar; and also for Jamaica to stop divestment before it is too late because that will negatively impact on the nation's economy and its future. Pray for exposure regarding the Martha Brae River and that entire area.

30. There will be a lot of betrayal that will take place in the JLP and PNP. Particularly, JLP. Pray that we will not have another Donald Sangster situation. There will be also switch from one

party to the next. Pray for all of the "higglers" within the nation. As there are plans to get rid of the "higglers" and to sabotage and kill livestock and poison the livestock to get the land. Pray!

31. The Lord says, if the NIDS implement in the present state people will be framed, stories fabricated, and it will increase Crime and Contract Killing. Rapists will have access to information from within - everything about the person will be exposed. Privacy will be compromised, even with the politicians. Many people will be tracked, especially those who owe taxation. Problems within the health sector: wrong blood diagnosis, issue from within, missing medical files, surgical problems, missing police reports especially regarding homicides/murders, tickets given for spot check, several surveillance problems, invasion of privacy. Politicians will use the information against other politicians. Nations, this is not a JLP or PNP issue, this is about Jamaica. It will create a credit system which will create greater suffering on the poor.

32. As nations continue to digitize, we will see more fraud, more hacking, more cyber-crimes and more trouble than we anticipated. The leaders also need to be warned as there are Trojan

horses within the Nations, nothing is safe. Be careful before implementation.

33. There is a great outcry for the Youth in Jamaica.
The enemy wants to take them out. The Lord says He wants His people to rise up from different parts of the island and cry out for the children.

34. Pray for the fishermen in Jamaica and throughout the nations. The must begin to arm themselves and also let the authorities know their whereabouts. They will be coming up against deadly sea creatures as well as pirates.

35. Pray for the entire Red Hills, and Red Hills Road. For they are building Jamaica for a fall. The Lord says, unless Jamaica repents, there shall be a fall. But God will take care of the poor and those who take care of the poor, as they have forgotten the poor.

36. God wants the people in Jamaica to cry out for God to reveal the hidden agenda, motives, and undermine behind the crimes in Jamaica. It has to do with power, greed, and control. It has to do with other agendas and sexual rights. The people must pray.

37. The government must put a system in place to investigate all resources that are given to NGO's in the nation. What is the source and

purpose? It is critical to the crime, violence, and destruction of family that is taking place. Is it to help life, or destroy life?

38. The Lord calling on all the spiritual leaders in Jamaica, who are truly His, to begin to take their members into the street within their immediate community to evangelize. Which includes small and large business. There has to be unity to combat the devil's plan. Also, the areas that they need to watch, Mona, Stony Hill, Mountain view, Westmoreland, St. Elizabeth, Hanover, Clarendon, St. Ann, Oracabessa, St. Mary, St. Thomas, Waterhouse, Duke Street, Portland.

39. Pray for Kingston Wharves and the Norman Manley International Airport. Pray against corruption and that things will not tarnish the nation. Pray also that disaster will not hit Kingston Wharves. Pray against an increase in contract killings.

40. The Jamaican Government is constantly requesting help from other countries for monetary loans, but the government has the resources at Bank of Jamaica. For example, the notes and so on.

41. The Reggae Boyz Team need to be more serious

as individuals and as a Team: each player is talented and needs to have his mind renewed. They need to see themselves as Winners each time before a practice and before a match.

42. The Jamaican Olympic Team needs more focus to discern when there is deception because many athletes from other countries are not pleased with them. They do not want them to win or to be recognized in any way. Be watchful, wise, and confidential because this goes beyond simple rivalry and sportsmanship. Be warned!

## Word For Other Nations

43. If the USA political administration both democrat and republican do not change from the direction they are heading, more people will become homeless. We will begin to see violence erupt, crisis, and chaos. The Lord is not pleased with the treatment of the poor. We will begin to see more disasters breakout in different states because of the treatment of the poor. [Proverbs 30:8-9]. Who are speaking for the voice less, the poor, fatherless, and the widow? Furthermore, the USA pulling out of Syria will cause a regrouping of radical Islam and a re-emergence of ISIS. This will put the USA in greater

danger and set a death trap for Syria, the USA and Israel.

44. God is calling America to unite, repent, and get back to the place; otherwise there will be more famine and disaster will hit them. be warn. For the Lord says, a nation is evaluated by the way they treat the poor, not the way they treat the rich. America must get back to the things that allowed them to be great in the past: Humanitarian and the Family.

45. There are plans to assassinate a world leader, and we must pray against it. There is going to be major shaking and shifting for countries that are building without God. Great surprises shall come from the North, South, East and West – worldwide. Even Russia is rising but will not last for long. Pray against an attack on Brussels, Belgium.

46. We are in a season where many politicians are implementing principles and policies that are negatively affecting the poor, the vulnerable and the voiceless. According to Proverbs 31: 8 – 9 "Open your mouth for the speechless, in the cause of all who are appointed to die. Open your mouth, judge righteously, and plead the cause of the poor and needy." God places leaders in position to help other human beings and utilizes all that lies in their power. But too many hidden motives and desires have caused

many to suffer. The Lord says His hand shall be heavy upon them.

47. Political leaders must stop bickering and fighting against each other. They need to be united and come together to deal with what is coming globally. Many of them have turned their backs on the poor. No one should be penalized because of the party they support when it comes to the distribution of resources. That is what has led to the increase in poverty. Unless leaders repent, God says He will drive them like animals out of their positions.

48. Thus says the Lord: There shall be a great turmoil in the east that cannot be quenched by man-made tools, because it is My perfect will. Also there will be weeping and wailing from the west. My wrath will be upon Turkey, Saudi Arabia, Eastern Europe, Palestine, Pakistan, Uzbekistan, Egypt, Iran, USA (especially Massachusetts and Kentucky).

49. Pray for Sudan, Denmark, Zimbabwe, Ethiopia, Bangladesh, India, Kenya (Nairobi). The Lord says that there are major vulnerability within Kenya's security force that has the potential to bring major disaster in 2019, and could force

them into un-Godly alliances to try and rectify the problem.

50. There will be more uprisings within the USA – New York, North Carolina, South Carolina, West Virginia, Washington D.C., Florida, Alabama and Louisiana (especially New Orleans).

51. Pray, because more disasters will be taking place in India, New Jersey, Boston, Kentucky, and The Carolinas. Pray also for the smaller islands in the Caribbean – Turks & Caicos, The Cayman Islands, The Bahamas, and all the other small islands in the Caribbean as well as Jamaica. Pray against those islands disappearing under the sea as a result of disasters.

52. Cuba, there is going to be a revolution, revival, and awakening that will break out in Cuba. God want His people to pray for Cuba as it will be a short window. Many strong hold will come down.

53. The Lord says there are going to be riots and demonstrations in Barcelona, the USA (regarding immigration). The current immigration policy in the USA that is being pursued will negatively affect both the economy and tourism; and will open the door for new

and unfavorable norms which would not be in the best interest of the USA.

54. There is a major explosion that will take place between China and the USA. It has to do with a married diplomat and politicians who are raping and sexually abusing young boys and girls.

55. 2019 The Spirit of Perversion will be set loose in and onwards to directly affect little children and teenagers across nations we must pray like never before. Sexual perversion will even take a new turn. It will be so rampant that even the non-believers will start to fight against it. Spiritual and moral foundations are cracking, so if the foundation was not right at the beginning it will breakdown. The Lord says, "Stop touching and sexually abusing the teenagers! They are valuable to Me!"

56. Pray for the Children of this world and against the attacks coming at them; the next generation is great. Many of the Christian parents and leaders have been slack and the children are at great risk. The head of the beast is now rising. All the plans for the last 12 years was a set up for what will take place in 2019.

57. There are many angels that have been released many angels on horses riding into the following countries because of the covenant and agreements that they have signed. There is going to be an explosion and a removing of the covers from those involved – The United States of America, Jamaica, Russia, Japan, China, South Korea, Norway, India, Yemen, Pakistan, Britain, Iraq and Iran.

58. Mighty ones will be displaced and their glory taken away because they refuse to serve and obey Me in Spirit and in Truth. The homes of the unfaithful will be desolate. They will persecute those who are living (right). I am about to do a thing in the land. Hearts will fail – ears will tingle for then shall the people know that I Am the I Am. I have been warning the rebellious nations through My servants I have chosen to carry the Word. You shall live to see My words come to pass and many shall bow before Me and repent; and if the great world leaders will not adhere to My words and obey them. I will remove them and show them a sign. I will reveal their hearts to themselves.

59. Many great leaders will fall and many lifestyles will fall in apostasy. God will remove the cover of many of the hidden lifestyles that have been lived of many leaders including church leaders. In 2019 we will see the importance of tithing.

Many leaders that are covering with things that are not of God, 6 major churches will come under serious persecution because of their lifestyle (EXPOSURE) God will not allow the life style that they are living to corrupt the young ones. The organized church, God is calling them, into repentance to change their lifestyle. There will be a pouring out of the Holy Spirit and we will see miracle, signs, and wonders, and never before. Many will wonder what this is in the earth. Many men and women of God will rise up and speak, thus sayeth the Lord without fear.

60. (Judges 9) There will be much betrayal and there will be a major stir, locally and globally. Particularly in Leadership/Politics - murders and other evils will take place, all for political power. The spirit Abimelech will rise, the spirit of Anti-Christ will rise. We will see the elect of the bramble rule. A lot of false leader will be elected in 2019. God. Himself, will allow a lot of evil spirit among many leaders because of their wickedness, (Judges 9: 2). There will be a lot of false leaders in different sectors and areas.

61. New leaders, secular and spiritual, will emerge. Samuel and David type of leadership will begin to arise. God is looking for leaders to rise up in 2019, after His own heart. For man look on the outward, but God look on the heart. Worry

not, Saul is dead. God, also, will restore leaders, that has once failed – as Mephibosheths (2 Samuel 9), Mephibosheth.

62. There are some countries that are seeking God secretly for help, and God will send help for them.

63. The Spirit of the Lord is going to shake down the economy of the US, Ja, Mexico, Guatemala, Brazil, China, Libya, Costa Rica, Trinidad & Tobago, The US Virgin Islands.

64. The Lord is not finished with the State of California. The Lord is calling the people within this state to turn to Him Now for He loves them, for the enemy comes to kill, steal and destroy. (John 10: 10)

65. There needs to be more systems in place for the poor that will affect a wider cross-section because more people are losing their homes and only some are benefitting. The Spirit of the Lord is weeping for the poor and there are testing times coming for more of the rich. Every Nation's Government need to put better systems in place to assist hurricane victims who lose their homes, vehicles, and loved ones.

66. Major terrorist attack brewing in India. Also, the Lord says that there is a new breed of terrorists being "groomed" in the Middle East that are cruder, more defiant and even more manipulative, and they are willing to shift from one gender to the next.

67. The New Mexican President has accumulated lots of enemies because of his leadership style. Many of their citizens will run to other countries for refuge. This present Government will be targeted because of fraud and murder. There will be riots into the streets-burning of tires, cars, vans and some buildings and there are planned assassinations. The Lord is about to expose all the Politicians in the Mexican House both representing left and right.

68. The Vatican (Pope) is urging one of Israel's enemies to sign a peace treaty with them – and if that takes place, then it is time to look up because it would be the sign of the times.

69. Nigeria will be under siege. Pray for them, and pray for the Prime Minister of France, particularly for their advisors and the covenants that they have established which will cause serious attacks. Pray that they will change their direction and philosophy.

70. The Christian Alliance for the African countries need to increase their fasting and prayer for solutions, and wisdom regarding how to fight un-Godly influences in the African nations in the government and from other developed countries that will pressure them to make un-Godly Covenant and cause oppression.

71. Global leaders must be careful of the source behind their advisors. Many of them, because of the advice they are receiving, will bring chaos (including Jamaica and the Caribbean Islands. They have refuse to listen to God's holy Apostles and Prophets. God does nothing without revealing it to His servants. Amos 3: 7)

## The Word On The Climate

72. There will be shaking, weeping, wailing, perplexity, remorse coming for those who reject God and His Word. Many will be confused and in awe. Many have blasphemed and it will be too late for them; and for them mercy is gone and judgement has come! God is calling everyone to go home and find a place or make an altar and cry out for what is coming upon the earth. There is a great emerging of false prophets, there will be duplication of miracles and great deception and great infiltration will take place in the Church. The deception will be great in this end time. (2 Timothy 3: 8)

73. Natural disasters for India, Jamaica, Cuba, Haiti, Dominica Republic, North America, South America, Sierra Leone, Egypt, and Japan.

74. More disasters will break out globally.
Hailstones will fall from the sky. History will change its course only those who understand God's ways will understand His doings. But in it all there will be greater collaboration and great healing will take place. More disasters will be taking place. Sand will be piling up in some parts of the world and this will cause water to be directed to different places which did not have water before, as a sign.

75. and More dangerous laws have been formulated
are coming to put God's people in bondage, but God will break them up. Some will come under the heading of Climate Change and Gender Matters.

76. More fires will take place within the USA,
because the treatment and the cry of the poor treatment have gone up to the Lord. God is reminding the rich that He is God. Pray also against biological warfare that may take place and affect many.

77. A time is coming where no country will be able

to help the other – because of the vast number of disasters that will be taking place. Scientists will have great problems trying to understanding the atmospheric conditions that will be affecting the earth.

78. We should pray over all liquid substances that we consume before we ingest them. There are things that are put in them that are not good for our health all because of greed. The Lord says that we must take care of our bodies because incurable diseases are on the rise of which many are not aware.

79. Many are sick in their bodies and the doctors cannot find the issue. When it is revealed it will be too late. These conditions come as a result of sinful acts and it will be difficult to find physical cures to deal with these spiritual problems. Pray against a global flu epidemic and against the spirit of infirmity. Pray against the oppressive spirit that is going to attack every nation.

80. Millions of fish will continue to die on a global level and contamination will increase. Also, be careful of the animals with which you mingle – even pets.

81. Serious Climatic and cosmic problems will take place. Many lives shall be lost in 2019 and many diseases will break out that will not only

affect the livestock but the inhabitants of the ocean. The damage and massive losses within the agricultural sector will be great and create serious hardships. Many crops will dry up and die, livestock will die. We will see floods and rains in some places and much of the produce will be destroyed; while in others, because of the drought that will happen, we will see famine. There will be major food shortage globally. We will see thunder, hail, fire, lightning and the signs of times will break out. Even some cities, countries, and towns will no longer exist. For those within the occult, the hands of God will be upon them heavily including those worshipping Baal, Isis, Osiris - the ones they believe are the gods of life, health, and fertility. Unless they repent, they will experience the manifestation of judgement at the hand of Most High God Who is the Supreme Being - the One Who rules over all the elements. Many farmers will want to give up and walk away from farming because of the challenges. Food shortages especially with fruits and vegetables.

82. Those with massive investments in the agricultural industry will suffer great losses as a result of the disasters and it will cause a massive shortage in food including, peanuts, potatoes and other vegetables. This will cause a major famine throughout the world. But, the Lord says, "If My people who are called by my

name will cry out, then I will show mercy, and My people will be fed during the famine. As they obey Me, worship Me and give their Tithe, they will be protected." Pray for all places where oil is found and all places where the drilling is taking place, as there will be many disasters. Most of them will crash and workers will be running frantically. It will cause an oil shortage and increase the prices significantly.

83. my

A great disruption of the earth has begun, for words shall not return to me void, but shall accomplish what it was sent to do. (Isaiah 55: 10 – 11) (Revelation 9) We will see locust, plague, and death. All eyes will be on Europe, Israel, the Middle East, Italy. Also, we will see boils, skin diseases, and plagues will break out. (Exodus 9:9)

84. a

Due to outbreak of global sickness, we will see shortage of pain medication. More disease will also break out in 2019. Medical crisis. **URGENT:** The Lord says His people shall read Revelation 9. Many nations will turn to God. It will be a kingdom move in 2019. Rumors of War. Study the names of Abaddon and Apollyon. There is going to be a lot of torment and plague. But the Lord said, for His people who are called by His name, as you obey God's will, God instruction, pay your tithes, and faithful in His house, you will be provided for, sayeth the Lord.

85. The hands of the Lord shall be heavy upon those
who worship the Sun god, the universe. There shall be a separation of light and darkness. Light and darkness cannot coexist. We will see the manifestation of the 9 plagues begin to impact the earth – climatically/cosmically, and darkness shall manifest within 2019, unless people repent.

86. There are even far more natural disasters including fires, tsunamis, earthquakes and hurricanes coming for certain states such as New Mexico, Kentucky, California, Georgia, Tallahassee Florida, Utah, Illinois, Alabama, Hawaii and San Francisco. Global warming has had a great effect on these kinds of disasters going into various places they have never been before.

87. The citizens of Montserrat need to find new homes into other countries because of the major volcanic eruptions ahead.

88. There must now be great preparation happening
now for storing up on food supplies of every kind, cases of water, juices, candles, blankets, towels, diapers (baby and adults) and items for

babies. It is also time for reaching out to others (particularly the homeless) with some of these supplies because the disasters that are coming will last for more than two days in some places (states and nations) - lasting effects that will be spoken of for years to come. These disasters come to remind us Who The True and Living GOD is and who we are (we are nothing without HIM). The Lord will use these climatic changes (there will be signs in diverse places) to get our attention so that we obey His voice, repent and turn away from evil because He has so much that is good and pure to offer us.

## The Word On World Finance

89. As social, print and mainstream media giants continue to censor Christian principles, God will raise up new players within media who will dominate the marketplace and favor will begin to shift. Many of the media giants will begin to merge or go bankrupt.

90. Companies that give grants to support abortion and gender issues and come against the patriarch-led families will experience a downturn in their organization and suffer losses unless they changed directions, such companies will no longer exist and go out of business. Even long-standing organizations.

91. If businesses and investors will not seek God for guidance regarding business and investing and understanding the times and season many will be blown out of the water. Many CEOs will lose their jobs as a result of lack of solutions. Furthermore, the following businesses/businesspeople will face serious financial challenges – Bloomingdales, Lord & Taylor, Vera Wang, Kohl's, Saks Fifth Avenue, Amazon, and Digicel; but Bed, Bath and Beyond will experience God's favor.

92. Unless the leadership styles of many leaders global change, and unless they seek God and listen to the people, many will be swept out of office and lose power. Major shift in the global economy and many will go broke and become bankrupt.

93. The Town of Tain in Scotland will see an upsurge within their economy. Watch China in 2019 there are schemes to directly affect the US market in unexpected ways.

94. Britain shall see a change within their economy (boost) because of the great shifts that have been occurring within the Royal Family.

95. The next two years there will be a paradigm shift

within the UN, EU, NATO and the Security Council. This will create major changes for the world for the next ten years in ways that may catch the Church off-guard if it does not prepare and listen to the voice of God. We must pray that God's will be superimposed in every area. Additionally, Great Britain's departure from the EU is temporary. Britain will be forced to make new alliances with the same countries for political and economic reasons.

96. The economy of Venezuela needs urgent help because there are many tourist who have become more fearful due to increase drug trafficking, murder and kidnappings.

97. and The US Government has plans to withdraw stop the delivery of benefits to the poor, and are not doing anything more to help them concerning jobs that will pay well. As they do so, so shall God's Favor be withdrawn from them and many of the decision-makers and influencers will suffer defeat.

98. The minimum wage needs to increase to $20 per/hr. Many people working have not been able to pay their rent/mortgage as a result of their low salaries. People have been and are being evicted at record levels and are forced to go to shelters, but the shelters are not enough

for the influx of families; disaster is imminent without the change. All 50 states of the USA need to agree to this, especially for the benefit of the nation's children.

99. Monies need to be used to build houses for the poor because the birth rate has been increasing within all Nations, and the Lord is saying that the citizens need to be valued more because without the citizen's votes, where would the Nations' Governments be.

100. The financial economic situation in India, Pakistan, Yemen, Indonesia, Croatia, USA (Kentucky) and Jamaica are going to take huge turns. The stock market and other investment schemes will crash, especially Bitcoin investments. Anything that is done not in God's foundation will come to naught.

101. The economy is ever changing and it is going to take a direction that most people expect. It will be shaken and there will be a small window for the poor to act. It will be a time to invest into certain stocks and bonds because for the next twenty years, they will be beneficial not only for the Kingdom of God, but personally as well. *"For the Kingdom of God suffereth violence and the violent takes it by force."* (Matthew 11:12). This

will be a crucial time for the Body of Christ to grab hold of what is coming.

102. So many people all over the world, especially the poor students (young and old) who have taken out loans for tertiary education, for business, home, health (health insurance that does not cover certain kinds of operations), debt consolidation (rent arrears, credit card debts, mortgage arrears) need Loan Forgiveness. Just as there is Asylum for certain immigrants (aliens), there should be an avenue for Debt Cancellation. This should not be manipulated for the Rich who may have $30 billion homes going into debt, but for the ones who are destitute (most times cashless). Once people are truly not able to repay their loans, loan forgiveness should be granted. There comes a season in someone's life that the Lord will allow such an individual to increase in every area of life and they will extend mercy where it is truly needed, "For whatever a man sows, so shall he reap." If they have Loan Forgiveness, then the Lord will have mercy on some companies. Otherwise, we will see many banks crashing and there may be a return to the Great Depression.

**The Word For The Body Of Christ**

103. We are about to see the zeal return to the local

Church and revival within Europe, Latin Nations and the Caribbean. "Anointed men and women will be travelling to and fro to hear My words - here comes the end." Pray for Mexico - God will raise up the churches like never before. There is a gate open for the Church to rise like never before. There will be a mighty revival in the Spanish/Latin countries including Mexico.

104. It is the end time and changes are happening rapidly. Many will be shocked to see some of the words that I have spoken come to pass. In 2019, even many of the critics will confess that I am God. The attacks against Christians will be on the increase. The tribulation in many of the countries of the East against Christians will cause the Christians of the West realize that it is indeed the end time. It is the time for accountability. The Lord says, "Woe to the Shepherds of the West that have led My sheep astray!" God is cleaning up. A mighty change is coming and it will start in the Church, because God will purge the Church in 2019 so that holiness be restored among His people. Many of the true churches are going through purging and many of the false shepherds will be exposed. The exposure will be so big that it will cause the masses to attack the Body of Christ. But the Lord says, "Hold fast to your faith and trust Me, for when the shaking starts

many who do not yet know Me, will cry out for the Lord,"

105. The Lord says The Church must be awake for the times and seasons ahead are perilous. Laws will be now put in place directly affecting the Church and its freedom and flexibility to preach the undiluted Gospel of Jesus Christ across the world. Every Christian across every nation will be affected and will face the choice of whether to follow man's laws or God's Commandments.

106. Pray for TBN as trouble looms.

107. The Spirit of the Lord says there is too much talk regarding "church hurt". Many have not gathered together with others in church and ministry but have instead chosen to stay home. The Lord says they must repent, receive healing and get back into the assembly. Remember 1 Corinthians 14: 33, "For God is not the author of confusion but of peace, as in all the churches of the saints." Also remember Hebrews 10: 24 – 25, "And let us consider one another in order to stir up love and good works, not forsaking the assembling of ourselves together, as is the manner of some, but exhorting one another, and so much the more as you see the Day approaching." The Lord says many of His

people have been hurt because they did not allow Him to process them.

**108.** Bishops and Pastors, do not enter into any (spiritually) unlawful covenants. Stewardship! God shall deal with the stewardship of individuals. What one sows, so shall one reap in 2019. We will see the manifestation of Revelation 13 and Revelation 17 in the earth. A lot of generals in the body of Christ, that they have served God well, will be called home.

109. God is calling on the Kingdom people to begin to do the things He has instructed them quickly as the Kingdom of Heaven is at hand. God shall honor the covenant He has established with us and our off spring. (Genesis 9:9)

110. As in Amos 9 the Lord is going to have the Praise and Worship that He deserves, and He will restore what has fallen so that His praises come from the heart of His people. "The time of division is at hand. I shall separate My people which are called by My name. They shall rejoice and be blessed. Many that have lost My love, but through My faithful ones they will be restored."

111. He is about to go through churches. Those who
are not living according to His will and in obedience will be separated. "Many have subtly

robbed My people. But I am with the poor in heart and substance, I will be their God and provide. There is going to be a change. With the wind of change on the rise, the doors will be opened for many of the true Shepherds and churches to move forward. There will be an influx of persons seeking God. Many workers of the Gospel will be needed to bring healing to the wounds that have been created by the enemy. Even governments will be reaching out to find true men and women of God and God's true Prophets. The stone that the builder rejected will become the chief cornerstone. There will be a turnaround in late 2019 for the churches and shepherds that were suffering.

112. says   There are swords are wielding and the Lord

He is going to cleanse the nations, "…Because they mocked My words which are life. Many are building private places to hide, but they cannot hide. But great provision is made for My people as they humble themselves."

113. There will be great deception. (Joshua 9) The deception is that leaders have spoken one thing and have done the opposite and have engaged in corruption and have hurt my people. The church must be careful of unholy alliance which will be a part of the deception to infiltrate God's people. May will come under disguise, God is calling His people to seek Him before forming any alliances in 2019. Many will

say they are coming from afar, but the enemy is near. God is calling the body of Christ not to trust in their own strength, but to pray for greater discernment as the deception will be great. Do not trust in your own wisdom. Seek the Lord in 2019 because the deception will be great towards the body of Christ. But pray for greater discernment, big things and small things, for the spirit of Delilah and Jezebel will reign in 2019. Know no man by the flesh, but after the spirit. Deception will be great, not only the body of Christ, but politically and the civil society. Many great men will fall in 2019 away in deception. Be careful of all covenant, contracts, and alliances, even some that will promise get rich quick.

114. 2019 is a time to build, a time to build God temple. Secular leaders who uphold God principle, and who doesn't bow to the system of the Anti-Christ, those who stick to values and attitudes, the Lord said he shall bless them. (1 King 9; 2 Chronicles 9). The leaders who have been building nation, and coming against the things of God, many shall crumble in 2019.

115. Remember the 9th hour of prayer my people, (Acts 3:1, Acts 10:30, James 5:15). Because of the unfaithful, to God's house, the neglect of building God's house, neglect on giving, focus on self, while the poor, fatherless, and widow suffer, have hindered to receive the blessing of

God. Unless they repent or put God first who is the secret of both spiritual and material prosperity. Unless they repent and turn many shall suffer in 2019. But those that are faithful, who follow His principle will never put to shame, they shall walk in abundance in 2019.

116. We will see manifestation of the Holy Spirit as never been seen within the Earth. Fire by day and cloud by night. God is calling His people to seek Him deeper within the Holy Spirit. How to lead the flock and He is calling his people to seek Him for both the small things and the big things because of the great deception that lies ahead.

117. For the Holy Spirit shall lift a standard in 2019, and God his calling his people for a separation of the clean from the un-clean. Only churches that are in alignment, (Deuteronomy 9), with the Holy Spirit will receive the inheritance. And God is calling His people in repentance, intercession, and to cry out for mercy. The changing of the guard in both the church and secular. We will also see the manifestation of the Beatitudes. (Matthew 9:3-11)

118. Widows will be blessed in 2019. There is going to be great persecution on the body of Christ, but God asks them to stand. Many false witness will rise, many prodigal will return. Also we will see the spirit of ingratitude, (Luke 17:17,

Matt 18:12). The pouring out of the gift of interpretation of tongue.

119. The Spirit of the Lord says many Christians have not yet recognized what time it is because they focusing on everything concerning themselves, instead of reaching out to the lost (poor in spirit, and the poor people who are without food, shelter, jobs, and finance). Reaching out to the poor and destitute in a genuine way is what touches the heart of God. There are so many Christians whom God has blessed with financial favor, but they are only concerned about themselves. The Lord is not pleased because we are burden bearers and we represent the King of kings WHO is LOVE and steadfast in HIS mercy towards us. The Lord is reminding us that when we give to the poor, when lend to Him.

120. There is a deeper place in God that He needs His people to experience each day, especially now, for He is about to pour out more of Himself to those who are still hungry for HIM. The Spirit of the Lord says there are too many friendly fires within the Body of Christ because everyone is not on the same page-not going in the same direction (some have allowed the spirits of jezebel, pride, gossiping, lies, anger, unforgiveness and rebellion to overtake them),

hence they begin to cause more problems. The Spirit of the Lord says time is running out and He needs everyone to be aligned before His Coming!

121. Beware of distractions, deceptions, especially from false prophets. The Spirit of the Lord is calling His people to discern, fast and pray, worship, and read His Word more in this season. Stay in His Presence.

## The Word For Entertainers, VIPs And Sports

122. Many VIP secular movie stars, VIP leaders, they shall be saved in 2019. They shall be a great catch. (Matthew 9: 9) The church must get ready for the big catch. Get ready, because some of the rich and famous will be walking away from their current way of thinking and will be seeking God like never before. God is going to bring change to a prominent person in the camp of the enemy and their change will cause others to recognize the power of God. Furthermore, regarding the Church of Scientology where much of Hollywood acting community attends, there will be many riots.

*North American Personalities*

123. **Queen Latifah (Actress, Singer, Songwriter)** – The Spirit of the Lord says the enemy wants to attack her health – unless she gives her life to the Lord. Pray for her health and salvation. It is time for some reflection concerning her lifestyle. The Spirit of the Lord has been speaking to her and she knows that she has to change and is worried what others will say. Queen Latifah needs healing and deliverance urgently. She is called to be a pastor but needs to receive salvation now.

124. **Justin Timberlake (Singer, Actor, Entrepreneur)** - The Spirit of the Lord says he has a lot of favor on his life but needs to be guided in the right direction both spiritually and naturally. He needs genuine people around him. The enemy has been attacking his marriage, family and finance. The Lord wants to get their attention, and he has to be willing to listen to sound advice. He wants to save his family and lead them to a good Bible-based church.

125. **Mark Harmon (Actor NCIS)** – Pray for his security, protection and well-being.

126. **Justin Bieber** (Singer) – Pray for his total deliverance and that he will not crumble under the pressure.

127.    **Omarosa** - The Spirit of the Lord says she needs
to surrender totally to the Lord now. She needs to forgive and allow the Lord to deal with the matter because this may cost her marriage.

128.    The Lord is calling the Latin Christian Music community into accountability. He called them out to make a difference and reach the neglected souls for Him. The Youth are dying spiritually, and He has opened doors through music, ministry and missions, but many have used it to win fans and fame. Many have conformed and have not been transformed, their minds are not renewed, and they are not allowing Him to use them as He desires. They have been granted doors of access to nations, but they are not focused on souls. The Lord says He called them out to be different, but they have instead embraced the way of the world. They are not seeking Him as they should to know what He wants them to do individually and collectively. The Lord is about to raise up a new set of Christian authors/writers, songwriters, singers who think outside the box and are not afraid to look beyond the world concept of how things are usually done or presented and step out onto the world stage with the new ideas and concepts the Lord will release to them. These are not looking for fans, they are determined to spread the Gospel of Jesus Christ and fulfill their purpose. They are

coming from the proverbial "backside of the desert."

129. A boldness is going to be upon the Youth and in many concerts/music shows, both Christian and Secular – they are going to demand more of the artistes because they will become weary of the routine. Their lives have gone unchanged and they are no longer interested in the usual experience. They too will be crying out for something different, something uncommon. It is the Lord's doing because He has lifted the standard.

*Latin American Personalities*

130. **Alex Zurdo** - Pray against attacks the enemy wants to launch against his marriage and family. The enemy also wants to execute a plan to distract and to shift your focus from what God has planned for you. The Lord is going to allow some friends to shift from around you, but it is so that He can take you to where He needs you to be for Him. The Lord is about to reveal some truths and he must stand and ask the Lord to increase discernment of spirits within him.

131. **Redimi2 (Willy Gonzalez)** – Discerning needs to increase as the enemy has plans to turn him onto a different path than the Lord desires. The

messages in his songs are about to change and the Lord says stand true to His Word.

132. **Bad Bunny** – God is going to allow everything around him to shake and finally get his attention, because He is chosen and there is a generation of youth that God wants to use him to reach for Him and for His glory.

*Sports*

133. The West Indies Cricket Team needs urgent intervention because some of their team players have not been happy with the running of the team. There needs to be one-on-one sessions with each player listening to each views/opinion and collectively. The managers and coaches need to employ some of these suggestions - they will bring great change, hence a win-win situation.

134. At the next Olympics in 2020, Kenya and Sudan
will be rewarded with medals more gold than bronze. The USA will have dominance in the next Olympics, but a few of their athletes will be tested positive for steroids. Britain, Trinidad & Tobago, Russia, China, Botswana will also do well.

135. There are too many athletes who are being

seriously injured from American Football and the Lord says this game has to be phased out. There are disappointing scores that the USA, Belize, Costa Rica, Brazil, Croatia and Uruguay will receive for the coming World Cup Soccer 2022. England and Pakistan will be competing against each other in the One Day Test Cricket Matches, but there is going to be something significant about this match.

*The Prophecies given are for 2018 onward. God can choose to hold His hand back from any form of judgement pending, subject to the repentance of nations and individuals. Jonah 3: 5—10; Exodus 32: 14; Jeremiah 18: 7—11; Amos 7: 3—6; II Kings 20: 1—11 and I Corinthians 13: 9. Please remember, God does whatever He pleases (Psalm 135: 6). He changes Times and Seasons; He removes kings and raises up kings (Daniel 1: 20—23).*

# THE PROPHETIC WORD OF THE LORD
## FRESH OIL (Yitshar)
By: Apostle Dr. Steve Lyston
February 25, 2018

**Psalm 94: 10** says, *"But my horn You have exalted like a wild ox; I have been anointed with fresh oil."*

We are in a season where fresh oil is being poured out, hence the word Fresh Oil or *Yitshar* will be at the forefront of our minds. We will begin to understand that the anointing is different from the gift. The anointing is what destroys the yoke (Isaiah 10: 27). Each time God is about to bless His people, He pours out fresh oil, new wine and grain! Furthermore, Numbers 18: 12 says,

*"All the best of the oil, all the best of the new wine and the grain, their firstfruits which they offer to the Lord, I have given them to you."*

So God will give us the best.

In addition to all this, we will not only be blessed on a personal level, but we will begin to see the emergence of the real church. Jesus Christ will again be the center of the Church and not man. It is not about man or man's wisdom. New desires will begin to emerge for the harvest – new lifestyle, new zeal and the Gospel – Matthew, Mark, Luke and John will begin to be preached again. People have become tired of the 'microwave doctrines', so evangelism will again be the order of the day and real prayer will be back again in our churches and schools.

There will be a hunger and thirst for Biblical Principles and Biblical Economics and a hunger for the supernatural; and we will see it in politics, government and business, and will bring stability to nations. Those who fail to embrace this Fresh Oil being poured out will suffer defeat. The superstar moments are finished as the Lord is opening the eyes of the people.

So prayer, fasting, feeding the poor and the manifestation of God's presence in the marketplace will be the new normal. A desire for holiness and righteousness will be stirred among the people – while a new prophetic voice will emerge, not focusing on material things, but one which will speak for the poor the fatherless, the widow and the oppressed according to Proverbs 31: 8 – 9 which says,

*"Open your mouth for the speechless, in the cause of all who are appointed to die. Open your mouth, judge righteously, and plead the cause of the poor and needy."*

They will challenge the Babylonian systems and the injustices of the day. Many of God's servants who have become weary and fatigued will be recharged, rejuvenated and restored, because of the fresh oil and the new provision that is coming. True laborers will come in as this is the cry of the true leaders! Cast your net again for a supernatural catch. Follow every instruction in this season and be sensitive to the voice of the Holy Spirit. Mass physical and emotional healing will take place as fresh oil is poured out, and nations who adopt the principles of God will be abundantly blessed.

This is the season to sow/give. Click on the DONATE button. Help us to transform lives and share fresh oil this season. See our work locally and overseas as you visit the pages of our website.

*Shalom*

# PROPHETIC CLOCK
By: Apostle Steve Lyston
May 16, 2018

It is critical for us to take note to see what is happening globally, particularly the Middle East and the actions that are taken by the United States of America which many countries may believe are unilateral actions. For example, we have seen the United States pull out of the nuclear deal with Iran and have become the first Administration to establish their nation's embassy in Jerusalem and at the time when Israel was celebrating 70 years of being recognized as a state. While many Presidents of the United States acknowledged and recognized Jerusalem as the capital of Israel – Presidents George Bush, Bill Clinton, Barack Obama – none was bold enough to establish an embassy there.

All these events have forced countries to take sides, thus officially revealing where they stand to the world. We have seen Turkey rallying the Arab league, expelling the US and Israeli Ambassadors. We have also seen Iran launch its attack on Israel from Syria. We are seeing the true colors of China, Germany and France as well. In light of all this, recognize that the Bible is being fulfilled right before our eyes. So, we are on the verge of two sides globally – the sheep and the goats!

The question is, with all those prophetic happenings, will we now see the beginning of the rebuilding of the temple? Will we soon see a false peace treaty being signed to coincide with the Book of Daniel? Or will we see the beginning of the battle of Armageddon? We must therefore begin to pray more fervently for the peace of Jerusalem as well as the Trump Administration.

We have seen where the enemy of our souls wants to fast-forward some things to bring an end to this Gentile dispensation.

**Why Is Jerusalem So Important?**

Jerusalem is the most important place on earth. It is the city of God, the capital city of the nations which God created by His spoken word. (Genesis 12: 1 – 3; and Genesis 13: 14) God made an eternal, binding blood covenant with Jerusalem. 2 Chronicles 6: 6 says, *"Yet I have chosen Jerusalem, that My name may be there, and I have chosen David to be over My people Israel.'"* Also read 2 Chronicles 7: 16; 2 Chronicles 33: 7; Psalm 48: 1 – 8; Psalm 125: 1 – 2; Psalm 137: 5 - 6.

Jerusalem is mentioned over 800 times in the Bible. God specifically said, in the book of Jeremiah, that those who fight against Israel fights against God Himself. (Zechariah 14: 2 – 3) So it is critical for countries that would pass resolutions or who take sides to take note of God's Word, that if they fight or condemn Israel, or try pass resolutions that come against Israel, or curse God's land or His people and try to divide the land, then it will impact negatively on their countries and some will come in the form of disasters, wars or even economic decline and destruction upon their own countries.

What nations should do is to pray for the peace of Jerusalem. Psalm 122: 6 says, *"Pray for the peace of Jerusalem: "May they prosper who love you."*

Countries who pray for the peace of Jerusalem will experience economic growth and development. We cannot come against God's plans purposes or even prophetic word. No man can fight God and win.

The Lord showed me the number 83 several months ago, which carries great prophetic significance. For example, new beginnings, birth, death, change, circumcision, resurrection, Divine completeness, perfection, the Godhead and restoration. I believe that toward the ending of July and into September, we would see Global change which may result in food, water and gas shortages and diseases would break out. So it is critical for countries to begin to **store oil, lamps, water, curtains, candles, blankets, flashlights, sheets, gloves, detergents, clothes, bath soaps, wipes, bleach, diapers, garlic, juices, Bibles, socks, deodorants, water boots, batteries, vinegar and lemon.**

The Lord also revealed through Psalm 2 that many countries are plotting against His people and want to employ the anti-Christ system against the people of God and particularly against Israel. But God will sit in the heavens and laugh at the calamity of the enemies of Israel.

## What the Lord Revealed

The Lord also revealed that there will be a global exposure – particularly with first world countries that try to accuse smaller countries of corruption.

We must also pray for the Royal Family.

The Lord is going to expose many diplomats and a lot of turmoil will rise in the UN.

There is going to be a global purging – both in the Church and on a secular level.

We must also pray for Spirit Airlines and American Airlines.

We must pray for India with great fervency – as parts of India are crying out particularly regarding poverty. Pray also for the protection of India's Prime Minister.

The Lord also says He will show a sign in Jamaica, but in all of it He shall protect His people. Many are worshipping what they shouldn't. He shall raise up new leaders – Prophets and Apostles as well. People should pray in tongues as never before and the intercessors need to live holy lives.

The enemy is trying to regroup. The Church in America should not be distracted and divided with race and political sides. They need to seek God to know His will and His ways. Many have become blind and are not seeing God's will and purpose. They should pray for the United States like never before and pray for the President as the enemy is trying to blindfold and implement a plan on His people. God wants His people to pray against the spirit of Jezebel. The enemy is after the church. The churches in the United States need to get back on the wall – there are dangers ahead. America, be warned!

# THE PROPHETIC WORD OF THE LORD FOR THE QUARTER JULY – SEPTEMBER 2019

## GET READY FOR THE STIR
By: Apostle Steve Lyston
September 2019

Times and seasons are critical – we are seeing a new season about to emerge. Everything will be stirring – from the weather pattern, administrations, businesses, finance, science, churches, agriculture, aquaculture – every sector.

Isaiah 19: 2 says, *"I will set Egyptians against Egyptians; everyone will fight against his brother, and everyone against his neighbor, city against city, kingdom against kingdom."*

Furthermore, Jeremiah 50: 9 says, *"For behold, I will raise and cause to come up against Babylon an assembly of great nations from the north country, and they shall array themselves against her; from there she shall be captured. Their arrows shall be like those of an expert warrior; none shall return in vain."* (See also Jeremiah 51: 1)

Stir means "to move, to shake to agitate, to change the position slightly or to displace; to arouse from sleep; to put oneself one's limbs into motion or activity; movement and mobility; to be active; to awaken." Things begin to come to life during a stir. Another definition for stir is "to move away from customary or unusual place or position."

The stir is causing strange and unpredictable weather patterns. The stir brings excitement for some and sadness for others. From it comes the word commotion. Stir brings different movements – the top goes to the bottom and the bottom goes to the top. Promotion comes during the stirring. When the times and seasons changed and king Nebuchadnezzar summoned all his advisors and required of them the interpretation of his dreams they failed. Their failure brought on his wrath and ultimate decision to kill those who failed, this was a stir taking place.

We have seen many advisors surround the king, and many advisors are under a covering which is not of God and are tapping into sources that are not of God. God is about to stir so that the true Daniels can come forth.

A stir has to happen in order to bring to life that which is dormant or hidden. During an earthquake, for example, sometimes the ground opens, water, gas or steam may sometimes shoot out; so it reveals what was hidden beneath the earth and oftentimes releases the pressure that has built up beneath the surface. Depending on where the stirring takes place, a whirlpool or vortex could result.

Within the sleeping church, many will be awakened! Some that have been given spiritual gifts but have not put them to use, God is about to stir them (2 Timothy 1).


The stirring that will happen will be God's way of shaking up things. Politicians will be stirred up against politicians for global change. God is not a respecter of persons. He will stir in order to accomplish His will – and help the poor, the fatherless, and the widow.

God will stir up the remnant to begin reaping the harvest. There will be a great harvest. God is already preparing the provision and the equipment for the remnant to begin to put on. (Zechariah 4: 1 & 6 – 10). God will pour out new wine and rise up a people to rebuild.

Many have taken God's work for granted, and because of that there are many of God's servants who have become discouraged in rebuilding His temple. This next stirring will remove the mountain and the hindrances coming against His will. The Spirit of Grace and Supplication will be poured out – however, not by might, nor by power, but by His Spirit will we rebuild.

There is a sound in the realm of the Spirit! Can you hear that sound! Those who are connected will hear the sound and will be stirred into action. God will stir us, for the stirring that will take place – global disasters will increase. Many are crying out for justice. God will stir it!

Just get ready for a shift like we have never seen before. Get ready for the return of the backsliders! Get ready for the eleventh-hour workers! Resources will come from unknown places, for the work God has called us to do. God is calling His people into a time of intercession and consecration. The drums of war are beating!

Take heed to His Word in Jeremiah 23: 17, Ezekiel 32: 2 and 13; Zechariah 9: 13 and 2 Samuel 5: 24.

# The Prophetic Word

1. Pray for England and all the British Airways aircraft. Pray for all the airlines globally. Pray for all those who want to give up. But don't just pray - extend a helping hand to those who need. You never know when the coin may flip. Those you see as nobody today, may be a king or queen tomorrow.

2. Pray for the following:
    - USA President
    - Prime Minister of Jamaica
    - Prime Minister of India
    - Former Vice President Joe Biden
    - Rudy Giuliani and
    - New York (especially Manhattan)
    - All Fivefold Leaders

3. All eyes will be on Russia – pray against military conflict.

# PROPHETIC PRONOUNCEMENTS!
## Prophet Passion Java vs. Prophet Shepherd Bushiri
### By: Apostle Steve Lyston
### November 4, 2019

The recent prophetic pronouncements and counter-pronouncements of Prophet Passion Java and Prophet Shepherd Bushiri have opened the door to confusion, controversy and division in the church particularly in the African region. Other prophets have joined in the throng to make their pronouncements in defense of their favorite prophet.

This event has brought into focus the urgent teaching the Body of Christ needs especially regarding the Prophetic Ministry. Many prophets globally, have even elevated themselves above sound doctrine, protocol and even the written Word of God, not to mention the operations of the Holy Spirit.

I am not hear to take sides, but to teach the Body of Christ about the protocols and the pitfalls we should avoid. Everything we do in the Body of Christ must give the Lord glory, and as such prophetic utterances must bring the glory of God not glory to man.

## Measure the Prophetic Utterance Scripturally

Every revelation or prophetic word must be measured with the Word of God.

1. Prophetic Words must be judged by two (2) or three (3). 1 Chronicles 14: 29 says, **"Let two or three prophets speak, and let the others judge."**

2. We must test the spirits to see if it is God, the flesh or the devil. 1 John 4: 1 reminds us, **"Beloved, do not believe every spirit, but test the spirits, whether they are of God; because many false prophets have gone out into the world."**

3. Personal prophecies are often given with conditions. They are also given to edify, exhort and comfort. 1 Corinthians 14: 3 says, **"But he who prophesies speaks edification and exhortation and comfort to men"**

4. Prophetic words must be given with wisdom, grace and there must always a window for repentance.

5. The receiver must receive with humility and test according to Scripture, to see whether or not the word is true. Furthermore, the receive should check the fruit of the giver. For example, find out if they are walking in integrity, are walking under a covering and so on.

We also see in Scripture where the prophet Isaiah in 2 Kings 20, delivered a word to King Hezekiah to get his house in order because he was going to die.

## Humility Required

The king received the word in humility and he wept before God for grace and mercy.  He never allowed pride or arrogance, nor did he hit back against the prophet Isaiah.  In Scripture, anyone who would cry to God for mercy and compassion, God always answers favorably.  God added fifteen (15) years to King Hezekiah's life.  He recovered from the illness and it is a powerful picture of how God always answers favorably when we cry out to him.  Although Hezekiah may have squandered the fifteen (15) years God gave him by exposing all the secrets to the Babylonians and caused subsequent generations to suffer.

## The Gift of Prophecy

Prophetic words are serious words.  The gift of prophecy may be misunderstood by many because of the abuse and manipulation for which many use it. Yet, 1 Corinthians 12: 6 – 7 reminds us, "And there are diversities of activities, but it is the same God who works all in all.  But the manifestation of the Spirit is given to each one for the profit of all:"

What has been happening is that some have been utilizing this gift for fame and popularity to draw people to themselves, but not to reach the souls and win them to the Lord.  Many are focusing on accuracy will they ignore the Fruit of Spirit.  We are now hearing of terms that are not

Scriptural such as "Forensic Prophet". I am still searching for the Scriptural reference, and I cannot find it.

## What Should Take Place

Let us say you are a prophet and while you are in prayer God shows you that another prophet or servant is going to die. The first thing to do is to seek God for further clarity to see if it means spiritual death or physical death. Then, with great wisdom and Divine Guidance, we try to contact the person – whether by email, mail, or phone call if possible.

If it is impossible for you to get to them, you can say "Pray against untimely death." You give the word in humility, not pride or arrogance. Likewise, the receive ought to receive in humility. The receiver should in no way look at the status of the messenger, or judge by fame, number of members in their congregation. God can use anyone to carry a message, including a donkey! He does whatever He pleases.

What if the devil wants to bring an illness or an airplane accident, or an accident of any kind? If they are too busy to listen, then what would happen. In writing this, the Lord reminded me of Myles Munroe. Could his death have been prevented? Were the watchmen at their posts?

Giving and receiving prophetic words should never be about who is more popular and who is more correct. Furthermore, the Body of Christ should not be distracted, but maintain focus on Christ, because He is cleansing the prophetic. We should never forget 2 Peter 1: 16 – 20.

No one should be declaring curses, but instead everyone should be in a season of repentance, preparing for 2020 and its harvest.

The Lord told us in 2018, that there would be a purging within the prophets of the African continent because He has given them much favor, but He has not gotten the glory! Many will be targeted and investigated for money laundering.

Recognize that, when one part of the Body of Christ suffers, we all suffer. There will be no winner when our focus is on who is more accurate or popular among the people. We need to draw close to God and He will draw close to us.

# 2020

# THE PROPHETIC WORD OF THE LORD 2020 AND ONWARD

*Given by the Lord through Apostle Steve Lyston, Bishop Dr. Doris Hutchinson, Pastor Michelle Lyston, Prophetess Nadra Brotherton, Prophetess Sophia DiMuccio, Prophet O. Onesto Jolly*

The year 5780/2020 is the year of **"pey"**. **"Pey"** is the Hebrew letter for the number 80 and is the symbol of a mouth. It is a time of great insight, breath, voice and Divine sparks of God. Moses was 80 when He brought the children of Israel out of Egypt. So, it will be a time of deliverance, strength and dominion. We will see the manifestation of 2 Chronicles 20: 20 take place. It is the Year of Souls. It is a time of Divine alignment as earth will begin to align to heaven's divine will and purpose. We are about to see the emergence of the Sent One – it is the year of the Apostles.

The year 2020 will bring the unexpected concerning good and evil, naturally and spiritually. It is a year that all Heads of Government will be visited by the Spirit of the Lord for the return of the Fear of the Lord shall manifest before them, and many souls will come into the Kingdom of God. It is the year that God's true worshipers shall rise and worship Him regardless of their situations.

Major shaking will take place, sudden release. A time of movement and shocking shifting. A great release of God's power and Presence. Major earthquake in diverse places.2

It will be the **Year of the Manifestation of the Kingdom** – a prophetic time. (Psalm 81: 10). It will be a year of decrees and declarations. (Jeremiah 1: 5). The Jeremiahs and the Moses' shall come forth.

States and countries not experiencing war, must now prepare for war on land, sea and sky. The enemy is about to descend upon those countries which are experiencing peace. This is so because the enemy wants the rich resources within. Laws will be imposed to deal with the evil when they are the ones behind the problem. Prepare for war! Watch out also for trade embargo. Travelers will become fearful but our faith in God will protect us.

There will be serious attacks launched within the Diplomatic Corps globally. It is internal and a serious shaking will take place with the potential to affect national economies and relationships. It is during this that many things will come to the forefront that will surprise us all.

There will be more apocalyptic happenings (Revelation 16, Revelation 5, The Book of Daniel). We will see freak storms, hailstones, floods and fires like never before. Store corn and wheat (Genesis 41: 49). The hurricanes that are inevitable to occur need not to be ignored for the upcoming year. Massive land slippage will take place particularly where houses are being built or where there are major projects. Some of those structures will disappear because of the weather.

Destruction around the world will be widespread on food of every kind, caused by insects, scientists will be confused because they never experienced anything like it before.

It is the **Year of Release and Recovery**, where the gospel will be preached unhindered. Knowledge will be released. Bondage will be broken, and many will be set free from trouble, obstacles, oppression, debt, hardships, oppressive rule, walls, and prisons. Manipulation, Witchcraft and such will be broken. Many high places will come down and unclean lifestyles will be judged. (1 Corinthians 3). Yet, if God can find twenty (20) He will not destroy the city. For those who are believing God for large sums of money, He says, "Begin to Tithe and I will bless you and increase your businesses according to Malachi 3."

It is the **Year of Restoration**, and some of those who were cheated out of their inheritance will get the opportunity to claim it back in 2020. Those who were deemed bastards – forgotten, are about to be remembered. The first born will be acknowledge and some will end up with a double portion as the right of the firstborn.

A great wind is blowing. One which will change the course of nature and of time. It will affect nations. It will affect organizations, (government and the private sector), international organizations, communities and families. This change will blow suddenly.

This is the **Year of Prayer**! Cycles of completeness and reward for those who wait. Jacob waited 20 years before his release and the manifestation of his wife and property. (Genesis 31: 38 – 41). Many things will be completed as it was with Solomon and more suffering will come to an end. Jabin oppressed Israel for 20 years before God moved him. This is the year the Deborahs and the Baraks will join together to defeat the Spirit of Jabin. There will be great testimonies of God's love and deliverance. We will see the birth and manifestation of many visions. It is a year where many strongholds, evil altars, oppressive and wicked administrator will crash to the ground. It is a year of being silent no more! It is a time of border expansion and reach. The limitations and barriers will be broken. The Word will be "Let My people go!" Pharaoh will be moved.

It is a **Year of the Unexpected**. We are going to see things happening that we have never seen before. Cast your net again for the Great Catch. (Luke 5). A visible sign will take place in the sky and it will cause many to turn to the Lord. Furthermore, a global oil shortage will take place and it escalate prices and affect the global economy. Pray for banks worldwide, some will cause hardships for people. There are some banks that will be investigated and exposed for their business connections with some Politicians locally and globally.

Paper currency will lose its value worldwide giving away to the plastic and bartering/trade of gold. But, the heavier the gold, the greater the value for purchase of land and vehicles.

There are Media wars ahead. The Spirit of the Lord is about to deal with the Media Houses for what they choose to present to the public. A great purging and shaking will take place within the media houses.

It is the **Year of Accountability** for kings and empires. Many will be dealt with concerning Tax Evasion. They have mad great demands on the poor, the fatherless and the Widow, but they themselves refuse to do it themselves. There have been too many deceptive practices hidden but they are about to be exposed; and those responsible will be held accountable. Administrations and Kings will be defeated and they will have to flee. There will be vacancies in every area of society.

In 2020, a great shift will take place God is reminding us He is the One Who establishes Kings and removes Kings. Those that were at the bottom will rise to the top and many at the top will reach their lowest points. The band of grace that many were under will be removed. The time has come for judgement.

This is the **Year of the Family** - the year that God will bless the families that are united. It is time for families to forgive so that God can pour out His blessings. Christian families will have to make some tough choices regarding their children's education in 2020. Many will compromise regarding to what they expose their children. However, every choice made in 2020 will be detrimental regarding family. The agendas of private and international organization will take on a forceful measure, but it will be up to God's people to stand. Now the sheep will be separated from the goats in the pasture; and the wolves will bare their teeth which they have kept hidden. God is calling His people to take a stand. Stand we must against all evil. Buckle your spiritual seatbelts. We are in for a crucial ride in 2020.

It will be a **Year of Redemption** and Giving – people will give resources freely to the Godly vision. A time of Maturity, Redemption, Ransom, Payback (Exodus 30: 14) It is the Year of Military Service and Priestly service.

The Year 2020 will be a **Year of Replacement**. Christian leaders who are not living up to God's standard of holiness and will not repent and change their lifestyle to live holy lives will be exposed. Hebrews 12: 14 says "Follow peace with all men and holiness without which no man shall see the Lord." God is angry with the wicked every day, but will forgive if they will repent. (Psalm 7: 11)

It is a **Year of Call Outs**. It is the year to build the house of God. (Leviticus 27: 3, Numbers 1: 3, Exodus 27: 10, Romans 8)

## Jamaica

1. A massive drug scandal is looming over Jamaica. It will also involve other Caribbean islands and will expose other operations and cause widespread embarrassment to many. The Lord says stop that operation now, look to Him and repent – whoever you are; your family will suffer and you will lose your dignity.

2. There will be great exposures coming for the Politicians who have been defrauding the people. Some will serve prison sentences for their crimes.

3. Pray for the Anglican Church and the health of the head of the Anglican Church in Jamaica, his health and all the Anglican leadership in Jamaica. Pray also for Lisa Hanna, Olivia "Babsy" Grange, Horace Chang, Gordon "Butch" Stewart, The Vaz Family, Christopher Tufton, Audley Shaw, Peter Bunting, Devon Dick, Julian Robinson, Mark Golding, Peter Phillips, Delroy Chuck, Pearnell Charles Sr, K. D. Knight, Philip Paulwell, Tom Tavares-Finson, Kamina Johnson-Smith, and Andrew Holness.

4. Pray that the government of Jamaica will not collapse before the time. Some will have to resign. Pray also regarding further in-fighting within the opposition that will cause further splits and resignations.

5. Tax Administration Jamaica (Internal Revenue Department Jamaica) will carry out thorough investigations concerning some Politicians within both parties regarding taxation. Many will be exposed, particularly those oppressing the poor.

6. JAMPRO - Jamaica Promotions Corporation is in trouble with its top-level managers – they no longer see eye-to-eye (dis-unity). Some are fighting for greater power and will do anything to attain it. This affects its original purpose/intent.

7. The basic and primary schools need greater attention. There is the need to show these little children more love, more assistance with assignments that will help by setting up an After or Day Care Program that will allow them to be placed into higher levels of learning. The Spirit of the Lord says many of them are missing out of academically and spiritually at this level, and more can be done by teachers, parents and the church.

8. The Law Enforcements JDF and JCF need to deploy more personnel because there will be increase in the number of drugs and levels violence within the nation.

9. The potential soldiers and police need to be vetted before starting any training because some of them are counterfeit. The armed forces in Jamaica need to undergo more training for what is coming.

10. There will be more celebrities worldwide who will visit Jamaica for its rich heritage, but our people must be vigilant.

11. Something good is going to happen in the parish of Trelawny regarding Tourism, as the people rise up in Trelawny there will be a great change.

12. As the people rise up in Hellshire and Port Royal

and expand on their fish businesses, great blessing will come to those within Hellshire and Port Royal – diets are going to change to eat much more fish.

13. The Sliding of the Dollar needs to be curtailed by the Government with urgency, because this will help to make the economy better. This will also allow more tourist within the country, as well as being an invitation for more outsiders to do business within the nation. Black Marketing is crushing the economy and should be totally eradicated.

14. The Spirit of the Lord says the interest rate on Certificates of Deposit, regular checking and also on savings accounts need to be increased in all Banks.

15. The Health Insurance Industry have not been giving genuine assistance to the people. Some people have passed on because they had very little coverage to take care of medical bills. Some Life Insurance Companies will also close down because their policies have not assisted with funeral arrangements as they proposed.

16. Bring back the JAMAL concept to Jamaica particularly for people in the streets who need the attention. The Lord says that it is time to break the cycle. It will help the children on the streets in particular.

17. A hidden and delicate document in Jamaica will be exposed. This has to do with finance surrounding both politicians and the private sector. Someone will fly the lid and expose it. It may cause death, but it will free the nation. The Lord says His people need to pray. The Lord says that what we are looking at is not what we are seeing, pray!

18. Most of the foods we are getting in the nation are contaminated and poisoned. We need to ask the Lord to consecrate the food within the nation. Ask Him also to consecrate the earth. There are chemicals released in the earth and in the water and also in the air and this releases many sicknesses.

19. The Jamaican Athletes for the 2020 Olympics need to be on high alert concerning their eating habits. There will be plots to bring them down. It is vital for each of them to safeguard their personal belongings and stay together as a group.

20. The Jamaican government needs to have low income homes built for the homeless, especially families, and proper provision of healthcare for

them that will assist them to receive medical care.

21. The Spirit of the Lord says He is about to expose
the oppressors of the poor and deal with them because He has seen the tears and the depression of the people, and as such many have become suicidal.
22. The hospitals in Jamaica need more medical equipment, especially for the treatment of cancer and other known diseases. Otherwise there are greater problems ahead and more people will die.

23. There are many businesses within the Plazas that will be closed because they are no longer able to survive with increased monthly rentals to pay. Pray for small business. Three major companies will also be closing down in Jamaica.
24. We must be careful as a nation as we advertise that "Jamaica is open for business to all!" This will create great problems ahead, particularly regarding national security. It will also create the environment for a web of espionage and a myriad of problems for the nation. Sovereignty at stake. Watchmen will be watching watchmen. It may also open the door for sanctions to be levied.

25. The Spirit of the Lord needs the Nation Leaders to truly repent and come before HIM with right motives to change and be willing to do as HE instructs them to.

26. The Spirit of the Lord says University and College students need to be given grace periods for the repayment of their student loans. If that is not done, more students will drop out and bring more stress to the nation.

27. The Spirit of the Lord says most of the Watchmen within the Nation are sleeping, and it is time for them to arise from their slumber to fast, watch, pray and sound the alarm.

28. Both Jamaica political parties are handing out guns, bicycles, chicken backs and rice in preparation for votes in the next election.

29. There is a major change coming for the banking industry within Jamaica. Other countries will set up their banks and they will not favor Jamaican workers.

30. Pray for all leaders and Members of Parliament in Jamaica as well as the Senate. There is infiltration in the land and it is unknown. Calling holy and consecrated men and women of God to come into parliament and break the curses that are causing the problem in the land

and that God can give guidance without a vision, the people perish! God will reveal all secrets -nothing hidden! Jamaica for Jesus!

## International

31. The results from 2020 US elections will produce
    shocking numbers that may cause a civil war in every state. People must pray for the US election as this one is critical. Also, there will be surprise votes in Richmond Virginia.

32. The Secret Service will come under close scrutiny within the US because of fraudulent practices over the years.

33. The relationship between Russia and the US will
    diminish because of great exposure that could further impeach the US President.

34. There will be great famine within all 51 states within the US and all experience this both spiritually and naturally and great devastation, but God's people will be covered.

35. There will be more wars among nations. In all of this, Deuteronomy 7: 13 – 16 declares there will be blessing and healing for God's people.

Ships carrying food/provision will be hijacked (pirates) and cargo will be taken away. Pray for Jordan and Gaza, war for lands, communication will get worse worldwide, infiltration will take place to sabotage trade around the world.

36. Money in all its forms will play a very significant role in 2020. Many who were considered on top will go through great turmoil – sickness, diseases, death, divorce and other shaking will happen to those who were given wealth but squandered their resources and did not use them as they should. Two countries will be in war over money.

37. Chronic diseases will be on the increase without cure. It will bring death and much suffering. Because of the sinful acts man has taken to himself, many will die.

38. The drug cartels are using different avenues to bring in their drugs from the top and this has affected little children and families. This is and has been crushing the economy and the Lord is about to step in.

39. Pray for all the railway lines throughout the USA and the World. A great deception is coming in the USA. Pray for all aircraft,

airports, ports of entry. Travel will become difficult.

40. Pray earnestly for California, Alabama, New York (especially Long Island, Manhattan, Wall Street and Grand Central Station), New Jersey, South Carolina (especially Charleston), Maine, Texas, Canada.

41. Different problems will arise out of Wall Street that will cause many to run into debt. Wall Street will bring instability in the economy.

42. The French Prime Minister will have many situations to solve because his own cabinet undermines him because of his age. There are plots and plans to overthrow the government.

43. The Ford Company will suffer huge loss in sales and lawsuits for mistreatment to their former and present employees. Pray also for Walmart – there will be a split which may affect thousands of staff members.

44. The USA/China relationship will weaken further, as trust is lacking and China is of the belief that they don't need the USA.

45. There will be major wars within Cuba, Venezuela, and Nicaragua that will have a domino effect to other countries.

46. Sex trafficking is on the rise and it shall be exposed within every state within the US and within every country, says the Lord

47. The Spiritual, Mental and Emotional well-being of young children of VIPs, Politicians, Diplomats and other Officials are being neglected, and a new generation of the "Latchkey Kid" is rising. We must pray for those children, because they are now also "armed" with limitless, unsupervised, technology, exposure to the sex trafficking industry, official immunities, money and the new thrust regarding the rights of the child.

48. Many of the Mexican people believe that they have been deceived by their President Andrés Manuel López Obrador because they have not seen the change that they have longed for and they are now seeing his true leadership style that are not in favor for the poor. (Serious problems ahead.

49. We are about to see the migration of large numbers of fish and mammal to the land. They will be running from the sea. This will be a sign. Experiments will also go wrong.

50. Pray, because major and widespread food contamination will take place.

51. Pray for the West Wing of the White House. There will be demonstrations throughout the US concerning health insurance coverage, new gun laws, and treatment from law enforcement.

52. A new level of evil mixed with the scientific are taking place. Pray and cover your families.

53. 3 Major US airlines will struggle in this coming year, two of which will bounce back but one will fully go under. 2020 will be a rough year for the airline industry. Pray also for all airlines beginning with the letter P.

54. Disney Cruises, Disney World and Epcot Centre will face lawsuits not only within the USA, but also worldwide.

55. The trucking industry will undergo a major shift that will negatively affect smaller trucking companies and owner/operators. There will be a great outcry for better legislation that the small people a better chance to make a living.

56. There will be torrential rains and landslides in Honduras, Ecuador, Guatemala, Haiti, Guyana, Grenada, Jamaica, Houston, Texas and Cancun, Mexico.

57. There will be Tsunamis in diverse places such as Turkey, Bangladesh and Guam. There will ALSO be desert storms in Egypt as have never been recorded before, for which many lives will be lost.

58. There will be earthquakes and fires in different places within California. God is not through with them yet.

59. Physical and Spiritual Earthquakes will be shaking cities and in the midst of the shaking, there will be frightening exposures. In the midst of the disaster, people will be running around naked and afraid during which infidelities and alternate hidden lifestyles will be in full public view.

60. More volcanic eruptions shall occur within Montserrat and Hawaii. Disaster will hit Japan and China. Pray for Iowa – fires will breakout. More floods in Istanbul.

61. There will be attempts to poison a globally known politician.

62. A leader will rule the USA and his rule will be hard to determine. Part will be good and a part will be bad. Many will be deceived. Some will be happy but ultimately Great Sorrow for all.

Only the righteous will be saved from the iron rule because they are led by the Spirit of God. A paradigm shift will take place that will change the world. Dark days are coming when many will refuse to eat. Many will die; some will commit suicide and this will also affect the whole earth. There will be famine for the Word of God, famine for the truth and famine for food. At the time appointed, that leader will change dramatically and those who support that leader will be disappointed. A leader will rise up and change things for God' people. Furthermore, there is a scandal that will breakout that will cause the leader to hide away. God will cover His people but some states will not recover.

63. Leaders in the Kingdom and secular world will pay for their deeds in 2020. God will not be mocked. As a man soweth, so shall he reap, and not just reap but reap double. As in Exodus 22: 7, there will be an exposure and when the thief is found, he will have to pay double. There are many rumors that were going around concerning management, leadership, and organizations, but now everything will come to light. Many will show their hand in 2020. i.e. companies, churches and individuals will take a stand to show if they are on God's side or not.

64. More cut-offs regarding food assistance will take place in the USA. It will lead to more homelessness. "Pray for the poor My people."

65. Immigration policies that the USA is now pursuing will bring great suffering and serious problems ahead. It will affect the family, the economy, the future and the Church as well as Real Estate, Education, The Army and cause homelessness. Those who impose it will regret it in the future and weep on their beds. They will make it easier for some and harder for the poor to enter the nation. Those they favor will not have any loyalty to the country.

**Entertainment**

66. Immorality by adults have left no proper values and attitudes for the future generation. God's judgement will be heavy upon the entertainment industry, because of their actions – unless they repent.

67. Pray for Show Hosts Wendy Williams, Oprah Winfrey and Ellen DeGeneres; also for Hollywood Stars Kevin Costner, Will Smith, Tom Cruise, Morgan Freeman and Denzel Washington. The enemy has been on a hunt to deceive the actors and actresses for their money and their life.

68. Pray for Madonna that she will not go into the asylum. Pray for Jay-Z and Beyoncé that they will seek the Lord for Salvation before it is too late.

69. The Lord says keep away from large, major private gatherings and places of amusement. People must pray wherever you gather at places of amusement. The enemy wants blood. Pray My people. Because of the attack, many will commit suicide. Stop your idol worshipping for riches and fame, for the Lord says revival will break out despite the evil and there will be a great harvest of souls. Many people will be saved.

70. The trend of collaboration of the saved and the unsaved in music industry will increase and so will the deception that comes with it. It looks like reaching the Lost, but instead is another bi-product of Apostasy. This will also open the door for increasing carnality within the Churches throughout the USA and across the West, particularly within Praise and Worship. Discernment required!

71. The Spirit of the Lord says Moses "Beenie Man" Davis needs to accept Jesus Christ as Lord and Savior. He is chosen to preach the Word of God.

72. The Spirit of the Lord says it is time for Reggae

Entertainer Beres Hammond. Pray that God will heal and save him.

73. Pray for Pastor John Gray and his wife there are serious times head and must revamp his circle of friends and associates. Must increase in fasting and pray. He will go through a time and stripping and betrayal, but God will raise him backup for his glory.

74. Tamera Mowry-Housley and her husband Adam Housley God want to reveal great things to them and they must seek God in before every business and personal decision. God wants to use them for his purpose. It's not business as usual.

75. The Lord wants all Gospel artists to revisit the way they do Business them must focus more of Their worship lifestyle, relationship with God, as well has their Ministry integrity.

76. The Spirit of the Lord says he does not know many of the Christian/Gospel artists because their hearts are far from him.

77. Chevaughn Clayton, the Lord says disaster is knocking at your door. Jesus Christ wants you to turn your life fully over to him now.

# The Church

78. There are troubling times ahead. We must pray for the Universe, the Body of Christ because there are things that will impact the universe that the Church is not ready to deal with. "But if my people only know the suffering coming upon the earth, they would begin to pray", says the Lord.

79. A great outpouring of the Holy Spirit will be coming on God's people that will cause a massive evangelistic mission around the world, causing many to accept the Lord Jesus Christ as their Lord and Savior before His return as in Joel 2: 17 & 28

80. The Spirit of the Lord says the enemy wants to completely bring the spirit of discord among the entire Family. He is also gathering all His TRUE Apostles and Prophets to embrace more of His Presence, to sound the alarm [warfare].

81. The Spirit of the Lord shall purge the false prophets in the year 2020 and above because the coming of the Lord is near, and they have scattered My people with their lies. Micah 2. Watch my hand in Africa, the USA and other nations regarding Prophets.

82. The Spirit of the Lord says there is a growing

need to pray for the children worldwide because they have been under immense attacks from within their homes, outside of their homes concerning kidnappers, pedophiles, Satanists, and many of them are attacked because of standing up for the right reasons, or at a gullible stage in their life. The children of today are surrounded by many things and the enemy does not like them. They have a purpose and they need to be preserved, for they are the future.

83. The Spirit of the Lord says "Woe to all spiritual advisors to the kings who have been luring them by their words for monetary gain!"

84. The Spirit of the Lord says "There shall be a great shaking within the Churches that are not of Him and have never been set on His foundation because they have caused many of My people to scatter!"

85. For those faithful churches that have lost members over the years. Do not fret. The harvest is here, and help is on its way. Many of the seeds that the faithful sowed over the last 20 years that seemed to be lost or on hold, will spring up quickly. The seeds sown will be repaid and the harvest doubled. There will be some transfers that will look sudden to us, but they were already in the making before the manifestation. For those in the Kingdom, great

men and women of God that forfeited and compromised, it will be time to pass on their mantle. For many faithful, who many have not heard of yet are waiting to receive their double portion and rights given to them by God himself.

86. Unholy organizations will cause many to lose your way, the eyes of God are watching you. This will cause sinners not to serve the Lord. God is angry with the wicked every day. (Psalm 7: 11)

87. Many well-known churches have now become "Gate Beautiful". Looks good but spiritually dead. The Lord says they must now come before him in repentance and pray.

88. 2020 will be a year of decision. Many will seek to change their lifestyle because the visible signs of the Anti-Christ will be seen and it will be an indication of the coming of Christ. The Lord says those engaged in evil must stop their evil deeds or else they will not escape the judgement.

89. The double-tongued ones will expose themselves. They will not be able to hide any more. They will need to make a choice. Some of those considered the elect will be deceived and make choices that will cost them greatly. Great men and women of God who forfeited

and compromised, it will be time to pass on their mantle. For many faithful, who many have not heard of yet are waiting to receive their double-portion and rights given to them by God Himself.

90. There is a serious global underground operation taking place. Only Spirit-filled believers will be able to discern the operation. A lot of global leaders are a part of that operation. This will cause many who are not discerning to be deceived and lose their way.

91. There are objects which appear and disappear in various places and when observed they disappear. They are spent on special assignment by a strange entity to undermine the work of God, to adopt a worldly lifestyle. Many have already been infiltrated. This can only be counteracted by discernment, prayer and fasting, living a holy lifestyle. The Lord says He will expose especially those who are involved. As Christians, we should have no fellowship with unfruitful works of darkness. (Ephesians 5: 11). Many will fall away in apostasy which will fulfill the prophetic utterance. We will see debauchery, depravity and degradation, particularly those involved in spiritual conspiracy. Christians, be warned and be ready for Christ's return! (Hebrews 9: 28).

Despise not prophesying! Take heed to your ways.

*The Prophecies given are for 2020 onward. God can choose to hold His hand back from any form of judgement pending, subject to the repentance of nations and individuals. Jonah 3: 5—10; Exodus 32: 14; Jeremiah 18: 7—11; Amos 7: 3—6; II Kings 20: 1—11 and I Corinthians 13: 9. Please remember, God does whatever He pleases (Psalm 135: 6; Psalm 115: 3). He changes Times and Seasons; He removes kings and raises up kings (Daniel 1: 20—23).*

# THE PROPHETIC WORD OF THE LORD
## January 2020

*Through Apostle Steve Lyston, Bishop Doris Hutchinson and Prophetess Sophia DiMuccio*

## S T O P!

There is a global burden for every true Apostle and Prophet with regard to the happenings worldwide. Many may not understand the season and continue to use the same approach they used for the last 10 years in this new season. The word is **STOP!** The Lord says you need to **STOP!**

God is disappointed with political leaders, business leaders and church leaders who have compromised and are encouraging secular leaders to continue to oppress the poor – passing laws which keep the people in bondage. Most have used their wealth, grace and favor to turn against the people. Every leader God puts in position – whether secular or Christian – He gives them conditions. Which include:

**Seeking Him.** 2 Chronicles 15: 1 – 2 says, "Now the Spirit of God came upon Azariah the son of Oded. And he went out to meet Asa, and said to him: "Hear me, Asa, and all Judah and Benjamin. The Lord is with you while you are with Him. If you seek Him, He will be found by you; but if you forsake Him, He will forsake you."

**Help The Poor.** The goal must be to make life better for the poor.

**Lead With Mercy and Compassion.**

Unless they stop and change directions, God will remove many leaders including Christian Advisors. God is the respecter of no man, and He will remove some administrations and some leaders suddenly. The only safe seat or guaranteed victory is for those who do His will.

The Lord says, "I will bring nations into derision who have dealt treacherously with the poor, and if they do not acknowledge My Presence and Me, I will remove them instantly"

"When I speak, they do not believe, but when I act, they will! But it will be too late for many. Millions will die spiritually and naturally. Many world leaders. Eyes will be open, but it will be too late.

1. A condition coming from the East. Viruses and skin diseases will break out. The East wind will take it across the globe. It will affect the skin so that there is itching and burning; superpower nations will blame each other for releasing into the atmosphere. Many will be affected and there will be a global cry for prayer to deal with the problems that will exist.

2. Major food contamination will take place. We MUST pray over our food before we eat it. Pray for the children and anoint them.

3. A popular global leader, their close friend will turn against them and it will bring exposure to a lot of things.

4. Pray for Thailand. There will be a tsunami. It will be the largest one recorded in that country.

5. The fire in Australia will cease, and God will get the glory.

6. God says He is going to bring a lot of countries to their knees that no man will touch His glory.

7. Disaster pending for Nigeria. Many will weep and mourn!

8. The recession will begin in the USA.

9. There will be an earthquake in Hawaii, Wisconsin, Texas and California.

10. A great earthquake will shake all the temples in Shanghai.

11. The hour is come – God will visit the Jewish people.

12. *"I am already visiting nation leaders in their dreams and visions, especially President Trump (United States), President Vladimir Putin (Russia), Prime Minister Andrew Holness (Jamaica), Premier Li Keqiang (Peoples Republic of China), and*

*President Cyril Ramaphosa (South Africa)."* The Lord says come before Him now, and seek His face for the interpretation for what is ahead.

13. God will be moving through Cooreville Gardens and Lionel Town (Jamaica).

14. The Lord says the Government needs to reopen the Monymusk Sugar Factory. This will produce more jobs for the people in Clarendon. Get competent and trustworthy people to run it. There will be a global shortage of brown sugar.

15. Unless Jamaica changes and repents, they will go through at season of great disasters.

16. Every spiritual leader worldwide must set their houses in order before His triumphant return. They must proclaim His name everywhere they go.

17. The Jamaica Defence Force must know that this is not the time for friendly fire. The greater war is on the outside. Prepare yourselves for greater war.

18. The Spirit of the Lord says that many are going about their daily life ignore what is taking place worldwide. Christians around the world should be crying out for the nation's being affected by

the coronavirus. There should be a National Day of Prayer and Repentance. The Lord asked the question what if He were to send one of us to China? Many would be fearful. We must remember that the Lord has not given us the spirit of fear. The solution is within us. God is bigger than the coronavirus. The nation needs to repent and pray. The Word of the Lord says "If My people who are called by My Name would humble themselves, seek My face and turn from their wicked ways then He would hear from heaven and heal their land."

## Get Ready For Reset.

In April 2020, the Lord said to give Him 3 years. A reset is on the way. People of God be ready. We do not know when God will come back and we do not know how He intends to reset. Hold on, 2022 will get worse before it gets better. This is the time to start making plans for survival. This is the time to seek God while He can be found. This is not the time to play church. Church leaders who made decisions without the directive of the Holy Spirit will soon understand and meet the consequences of their actions. Woe to the Shepherds that led their flock astray. Woe to those that sold out and listened to the wisdom of men stead of God. Those that trusted in horses and Chariots will fall but those that Trust in God will stand firm.

Seek the Lord for solution children of God. For there is always a solution. Some of God's children are still thinking within the box and looking for their solutions in the ways of old. There is a new way of life.

The word and wisdom of God will seem like foolishness to those that do not truly believe in Him. There will be persecution against His word. However, time will tell; but when the truth shows up, do you want to be caught off guard? I see a large mountain crumbling. I see destruction but with it, exposure. The Lord wants his people to study and have hope in Revelations 14. The Lord is coming.

## Jamaica

The Government of Jamaica made some very grave decisions that will cost them financially, socially and spiritually in 2023. These decisions will gravely affect the health sector and economic sector. Many church leaders and business sector leaders had joined forces with the government for financial gain. This was done at the cost of the lives of the average citizens. Even those that thought they knew what they were getting themselves into are going to be shocked.

2022 marks the year of serious labor pains for not only Jamaica and the USA but all over the world. It will take the grace of God for even the elect to stand. However, a great change is coming forth. While man is planning, God is wiping out. In the midst of a boom for some parts of the economy a turnover will take place.

The guards assigned to earth form heaven is slated to change in February 2022 and again in August 2022. The world will be tested even more. God is saying to his people, be sure to be hold on tight, be sure to be connected to me. There is a pruning that must take place. Many are set to gain the world and lose their souls. As I sieve, some are falling through.

God is shortening the day for His Elect. Yes, you will see the lost of lives of some of God's people, but to be absent from the body as a child of God is to be present with God. However, there are two sickles that are in rapid operation. These are the sickle of God and the sickle of the Enemy. There is a great reaping taking place. Which Vineyard do you belong?

Watch of Russia and China in late 2022 and early 2023. The news coming from these areas will shake the world. Also, the USA will take some bold moves at the in 2023. These plans were always in place, but it will manifest in late 2022.

Pray for India, Pakistan, Bulgaria, Haiti, London, and Ireland.

# 2021

# THE WORD OF THE LORD FOR THE THIRD QUARTER
## July 2021

We shall see shifting and shaking like never before; every sector shall experience the shifting and the shaking; and strongholds shall come down. We will also see many things shifting worldwide. Statues and temples will be shaken and shall be as a sign to the peoples. Major changes and shaking shall come to the governments of Jamaica, United States, Mozambique and India. The Church in Jamaica must be prepared for what is coming. It will cause great revival in the country. The gospel will be preached throughout the country.

There are many contracts being established by other countries to stomp out corruption, but it will in turn and shift to another class of people and the corruption will become greater within Jamaica and the Caribbean as many leaders and nations globally continue to build without God. It will be as it was in the Scriptures "...MENE, MENE, TEKEL, UPHARSIN. This is the interpretation of each word. MENE: God has numbered your kingdom, and finished it; TEKEL: You have been weighed in the balances, and found wanting;" (Daniel 5: 25 – 27)

The Lord says:

1. More airlines will merge.

2. We are to pray for the salvation and health of the US President

# For Jamaica's Olympic Team

They should not take this Olympics as lightly as other times, because a lot of turbulence and surprises will take place with different countries. There will also plots and sabotage, particularly the Jamaican athletes. Jamaican athletes should not believe that they are safe and take everything for granted. They must not approach the Olympics with arrogance and pride. There will be many with a vendetta against the Team, so they need to pray and fast and avoid eating from anyone. They should have their own chef and avoid eating out. This will also save them from stomach issues and other problems that can stop them from competing. There must be a lot of prayer and fasting. Additionally, the 4 X 4 relay women's team needs a lot of help.

# For Jamaica

We are to pray for Jamaica like never before as there are serious problems ahead. War will break out, and gun men. Many will be armed with high-powered weapons; the police will be crying for help. They will say "we need a plan." They will also go after the high-profile politicians who have been giving them the guns over the. NO ONE WILL BE SAFE IN THE NATION UNLESS GOD INTERVENES AND PROTECTS.

In Jamaica there will be a stir within both political parties. The older set will be "pouring the fuel" while the younger set will be "striking the match and starting the fire." The younger ones will begin to rise up and takeover. Many will be saying that they regret certain political decisions they have made over the years.

As in 1 Kings 22 – the Church will experience a great shaking. The state of the nation is a reflection of the state of the Church. Many of the global happenings are fueled by the actions and decisions of those in positions of authority in the nations including the Church. What we are seeing happen within the nations is the result of the actions of Church Leaders, as they have been giving lying advice to the politicians for fame and fortune. Many have mocked the warnings given over the country. They have come against God's true word. They have compromised for finance and fame and to maintain access. But the Lord says that in accordance with the scripture, we shall see the manifestation; a wind will blow them right out of the water and they will be scattered.

FAMINE IS AHEAD! The globe needs to prepare for the famine!

# THE PROPHETIC WORD OF THE LORD FOR THE QUARTER
**March 2021**

We are in a time and season wherein we are seeing a shift taking place. Every sector is being shaken while God is perfecting His Church. He is calling the Body of Christ to be holy, faithful, steadfast and have continued persistence in prayer. This is the time that the Body of Christ must be loyal. While many will be tested to see whether or not they are loyal to Christ. God will make a way to deliver as they continue to carry the cross.

We are in the eleventh hour, and so God is calling His people to rise. The anti-Christ is gaining ground because God's people have become lukewarm and have been sleeping. A global shaking is about to take place. Things will never be the same. The usual way of governing will be shaken. (Matthew 20: 6 – 9)

As the world continues to focus on COVID-19, the Body of Christ must prepare and be ready to minister spiritually to doctors and nurses. Many will fall into depression because of the stress and many will get sick after taking the vaccine.

## Jamaica

Jamaica is going through one of the greatest political and religious deception. It will be too late for many. Many have already sold out Jesus for the proverbial "thirty pieces of silver".

Pray for all orphans and golden agers and the children in the homes throughout Jamaica as there is a plot to use and destroy them.

Jamaican Travel Service business in trouble and will shut down.

There will be major changes in the ministry of labor in Jamaica.

Pray for the following Jamaican Entertainers for their time has come to use their talents for His glory, and the time has come to receive salvation. Pray for:

- Shabba Ranks
- Shaggy
- Mutabaruka
- Beres Hammond
- Scarface
- Bounty Killer
- Supercat
- Scorpion
- Ninja Man
- Dillinger
- Beenie Man

The time has come for them to surrender now before it is too late.

Pray also for Pepsi Jamaica, FGB (financial institution)

## International

We must pray for President Biden, the White House and the entire Washington DC. There is going to be significant in-fighting among the Democrats, and many will want the President to go.

Pray against a sex scandal repeat in the White House.

Pray for all the US Embassies worldwide and pray against attacks.

Pray for the Prime Minister of South Africa. Documents will be revealed which will cause problems among the people.

Pray for India. There are serious problems ahead for them.

As a result of the interference of the scientific community with the sun, we may see a global heatwave from which many will die. It will also cause famine and bankruptcy. We should watch the months of April to December. But the Lord says if the Church cries out in repentance according to 2 Chronicles 7: 14, water will flow and He will heal the land. There will be drought and lack of water globally. (Zephaniah 2 & 3)

Pray for the Vice President of the USA as frustration and undermining increase. She will find out that she was being used. Pray also for her marriage.

Pray for The Pentagon as great confusion and betrayals are looming.

Pray against electrical blackouts in New York and other states which may cause violence to breakout. Brooklyn is in trouble, pray for them. Pray especially for the poor the fatherless and the widow. New York should also make way for a new governor.

Many Airlines will be shutdown.

Pray for Kanye West as he is about to go through some very trying times. The wife will regret the divorce if she pursues it. She will go through a various painful time.

Jamaica's Accountant General and Contractor General will have serious disagreements which will bring great exposure. Unless Coney Island remains closed, there will be serious problems ahead.

Pray for the French Prime Minister, there is a plan to overthrow him.

Pray for Bishop T.D. Jakes as there will be a lawsuit looming that is to take him down.

Pray against any attempts regarding the Pope.

God will deal with Washington DC. Any laws put in individually or collectively, which are not of God. God will deal with it. Furthermore, New York and California will see shakings like never before.

# THE PROPHETIC WORD OF THE LORD
**Bishop Dr. Doris Hutchinson**
**Received April 3, 2021**

There are serious things will be happening on the face of the earth. Serious things are about to happen.

Every child of God must be ready in this season

Many were serving God but fell.

We must take the lead – carry the mandate that God has given us.

A disaster is going to hit this world that is going to shake everyone in the world.

We ought to be standing before God ready to go. This is a season of readiness.

Children will be walking out of their parents' homes and the parents will not know where to find them.

Leaders of nations will be in serious trouble. Some will be losing it!

Saints be ready! Preach God's word and live the life (holiness). We are in a blessed time because we are seeing the fulfillment of Scripture before your eyes.

Get rid of secret idols – cleanse your house and stay in the presence of Almighty God. Keep your house (heart and being) clean and pure.

Many Christians are wasting their time – be careful.

Pray for Kurt Carr, Vicki Yohe, that a revival will come to each of their souls and that healing will take place.

Pray for the Indian Prime Minister – for his health, security and the protection of His Family.

War will break out in the USA, China and Jamaica. God wants His people to be ready. Many politicians in Jamaica will get the COVID-19 virus unless they repent and turn from the direction they are going. The Lord says, "Too many lies and deception!"

The Real Estate industry in the USA will go through another storm and shaking, but, in the midst of that God's people who are faithful will be land possessors again.

Pray for Saudi Arabia, especially the crowned prince. A sensitive document will be revealed and get into the wrong hands, which will create problems.

God will visit the Jamaican Prime Minister in his sleep to show him the danger ahead. The choices and the decisions they are making will cause the people to suffer greatly. Also, 2 prominent politicians will experience health issues.

Many movie directors will be going into politics – in the USA, Africa and Southeast Asia.

The people in China are going to rise up and there are going to be demonstrations and problems.

Pray for the following:

- Sizzla
- Shaggy
- Tiger
- Jimmy Cliff
- Bounty Killer
- Beenie Man
- Sean-Paul
- Faye Ellington
- Cliff Hughes
- Usain Bolt

Pray for God's intervention in their lives.

There is going to be a spiritual revival in the marketplace with Christians, and they will no longer be afraid to praise God on the Job. The Holy Ghost fire is going to burn and they will be able to shout "Hallelujah" again without fear.

The Barbadian Prime Minister will make an announcement which will shock many, which will work in the interest of China. We need to pray for Barbados as they are in serious trouble.

As the flag of the Holy Spirit rises, God is shaking nations. An earthquake will shake and the Temple Mount will be shaken.

Pray for the Caribbean as a time of disaster is ahead. The Lord revealed, inundation and dislocation concerning Caribbean islands.

Famine, flood, earthquake and typhoon-like disasters ahead.

The Lords says there will be great shaking taking place at airports globally – both spiritually and naturally!

Shaking in governments globally – both spiritually and naturally. Many Jews will take the streets with their shofar and tallit as a revival will begin to break out among them.

Pray for the Royal Family as more problems will arise and more people will be sick with the COVID-19 virus.

Hospitals will be calling the Church to come in to pray because of the breaking out of diseases and plagues about to take place.

The Lord says those who were studying in the University will not be able to use what they studied in daily life application, as the level of disasters that will be taking place will force them to change their field of study. Many buildings will be closing. The Lord says most of them will be forced to work from the streets.

A lot of demonstrations will take place before the UN buildings in Geneva and New York.

There are going to be many demonstrations on the streets all over the world.

They will try to revive the Cruise Ship industry by targeting those who have already taken the vaccine. However, it will backfire.

Pray for owners of the Chinese restaurants as many more of them are going to close.

There is going to be a new surge of the coronavirus among those who have already taken the vaccine. Many will regret taking it. There will also be much in-fighting, sabotage and conspiracy among politicians globally. Some will be poisoned.

Many stadiums will close down and planned events cancelled because of the spike in COVID-19 cases. The US will impose more travel bans on countries because a disease will breakout. This will stop many Americans from returning home. Many of the disease are not being spread among the regular citizens. It is being spread within private clubs, hotels, private aircraft, transportation and supermarkets.

Pray for the police personnel in Jamaica as the Lord has revealed that many of them are not living right morally, which is impacting families and crime.

Pray against a tsunami hitting Malawi.

We need to be in the Secret Place, the Upper Room of the Most High God.

## To All

"Come and get it!"

In what ways are we thirsty?

How can knowing Him Who is Faithful at all levels help us today?

You have me always but are your souls still thirsty for me now and every day? I am exhaustless spring to run to. My water is free! There is no monthly payment; and other streams are dry and costly.

The Latter Rain is in the upper room, and it promises to water us with His Word. The Latter Rain represents the end time for which He has been preparing us.

We need to present ourselves to Him in a special place, because we have the Promise of Him not leaving us nor forsaking us; and we shall have His perfect peace.

**Scripture: Isaiah 55: 1 – 6**

Some think HE has gone silent on them, but He has not; He has been watching to see how much you wanted Him. He was testing our hearts to see if we would remain in right standing with Him or thirst for the things that are temporal.

There is a ring operating in Jamaica's 14 Parishes that have been recruiting and using boys, promising them a lot of money and it has been contributing to the crim and violence in the nation and the Lord says it must stop now! The young people are being destroyed for money.

The Spirit of the Lord says that there is a country that is subtly using Jamaica to establish covenants with an African nation. This will backfire and cause serious problems for the nation. The nation's leaders and decision-makers need to seek the Lord before they get into agreements.

The Lord wants the world to prepare for the next plague that will breakout in the form of a skin disease. We need to watch out for the Japanese hornets. They will fly in great groups.

# GLOBAL SHIFT AND HARVEST
By Apostle Steve Lyston
June 16, 2021

Most of the happenings worldwide have shown us the failure of the leaders at various levels throughout the globe to deal with the needs of the people. Many are starving because of the policies imposed during the COVID-19 Pandemic – and this as a result of the fact that leaders fail to seek and listen to God in building. So instead, they continue to build on sand. (Psalm 127; Matthew 7).
1 Corinthians 7: 13 – 14 clearly outlines the solutions in times of problem.

## Shifting And Shaking

Our global leaders hastily embrace the anti-Christ resources that brings nations further into bondage and famine and ultimately affect the sovereignty of most nations. As the global shifting and shaking continues, we will continue to see the relocating and restructuring of families for Kingdom purposes. It is critical for God's people to be sensitive to His move and move with His Spirit. It is a season for the renewal of the mind. The blessings of each person will be tied to the Kingdom. God is about to judge the marine kingdom and

## Harvest

Matthew 13: 24 – 30 tells us that we are in a time of one of the greatest harvests. In this current harvest we see the wheat and the tears being separated. We are also seeing the manifestation of the five wise and five foolish virgins.

The Bible speaks of many harvests including the harvest of souls, the harvest of miracles and rewards for one's deeds, and the harvest of finance.

We must recognize that during a harvest, we will need to work double time. In harvest time, there will be wars, because the enemy wants to steal our harvest. So, it is critical for us to continue to plant, reap and store. In reaping, we receive some thirty, some sixty, and some a hundred-fold. We are moving into the manifestation of the thousand and ten thousand-fold.

Harvest is something for which we have to prepare. Many believe that the harvest will simply fall into their laps. A person must have faith in order to reap during the harvest season. A farmer does not necessarily wait for perfect weather to plant, he plants regardless of what weather as long as it is within the right season. (Ecclesiastes 3) We don't go according to the world's ways, whether good or bad. The way of the world is finished.

# Know The Season of Your Harvest

Every farmer needs to know the season – when to check the maturity of the harvest. In order to do that, there are some things we need to understand about the maturity of the harvest.

When something is mature/ripe, you can see it, feel it, smell it and it sometimes falls from the tree. It has a specific color when it is mature. We must ensure that we do everything to protect our harvest. We must not complain because that kills the harvest. Tithing must continue during the harvest. It protects the harvest. Your tithing is your best pest controller. Many will come to swipe the harvest, but your tithing will rebuke the devourer for your sake. It will also open the windows of heaven and send rain. It will stop predial larceny.

Remember, in times of harvest, we must allow the Lord to lead the reaping. There will be wheat and tares, so there will be exposure during the harvest. God is the One who will root out the false and the fake. The tares can be false doctrines, false teachers, the Judases, the enemies, the goat and only God has the wisdom to do the uprooting. There are many times people will be in your vineyard as a sleeper/undercover, and only God is able to deal with them. So, we must pray to ask Him to purge and protect the vineyard.

We must have high expectations and patience during harvest. Many have sowed and toiled but this is the time of harvest. It can be your healing, the mending of some relationships and restoration. It can also be babies being born, gifts and talents coming forth; promotions, favor for the starting of your business, honor and reward for the good work you have been doing over the years.

This is the time of harvest for you!

# END-TIMES AND SIGNS EVERYWHERE
By Apostle Steve Lyston
June 16, 2022

Matthew 24: 3 and 7 says "Now as He sat on the Mount of Olives, the disciples came to Him privately, saying, "Tell us, when will these things be? And what will be the sign of Your coming, and of the end of the age? ... nation will rise against nation, and kingdom against kingdom. And there will be famines, pestilences, and earthquakes in various places."

We are seeing the manifestation of these words right before our eyes. There are signs everywhere and rapid manifestations. We are seeing the falling away of saints, which is apostasy, happening in every direction. We also see the church embracing a "death culture" and satanic doctrines. We see signs in the weather pattern including record-level, earthquakes, famines, pestilences and increasing global deception, particularly in the area of health and sciences. There is great lack of trust in God which has led to millions falling into scientific deception. Most say they have taken the vaccine for a better future (or so they think). We have seen the LGBTQ+ expand and many churches and nations have facilitated and bowed to their bidding for monetary gain. Churches are partnering with evil organizations, and the spirit of mammon have taken over nation leaders and some within the body of Christ. Many Christians have turned their backs on God for money. Many prophets have become religious in their thinking. Our weather patterns throughout the globe has changed drastically. Aren't these signs everywhere?

## Social Media and Networks

Matthew 24: 14 says, "And this gospel of the kingdom will be preached in all the world as a witness to all the nations, and then the end will come."

The pandemic has accelerated this prophecy. Zoom and other such platform have connected and continue to connect people globally, which is causing that Word to be fulfilled. Evangelists no longer have to physically enter a country in order to spread the gospel. The introduction of Artificial Intelligence (AI) has created a borderless global society in which to do business. It will be interesting to see what will happen with the Airline Industry.

The global pandemic has caused millions of churches to be closed – some by persecution, some by way of fear. In the West, many Pastors are being jailed as they defend their religious rights; while politicians are proudly glorifying the things of darkness. Aren't these signs of the end-time?

We are now seeing a new level of deception hitting earth. Some are offering "opportunities" to enter the lottery by taking the "jab"/(vaccine). Some are being offered the equivalent of less than a night's dinner to take the vaccine while the poor the fatherless and the widow are dying of hunger and neglect, and furthermore, no other sickness really matters.

We are now seeing some of the greatest deceptions in the pharmaceutical industry. (Revelation 18)

Recognize that Revelation 18: 23 says "The light of a lamp shall not shine in you anymore, and the voice of bridegroom and bride shall not be heard in you anymore. For your merchants were the great men of the earth, for by your sorcery all the nations were deceived." This scripture was in reference to Babylon, and the word "sorceries" here is translated from the Greek work "pharmakeia" from which we get the word English word "pharmacy." So this industry today fights against God-given, natural, simple remedies and are making enormous sums of money doing so.

Revelation 13: 16 – 17 reminds us, "He causes all, both small and great, rich and poor, free and slave, to receive a mark on their right hand or on their foreheads, and that no one may buy or sell except one who has the mark or the name of the beast, or the number of his name."

It is practically historic that today, nurses in Christian hospitals, policemen, soldiers and other essential personnel are being denied certain salient services and are in fact being forced out of their jobs because it is now mandatory (although silently stated) that they take a vaccine. Banks are also included in this web of deception. Aren't these the signs of times?

## Mainstream Media

We are now seeing the global power of mainstream media censoring and banning anyone who does not agree with nor share their points of view. Algorithms have been set to pick up on certain key words and phrases they have determined, in order to censor and block certain persons and groups they don't like.

Politicians are being reverted from key decision-makers and influencers, to marketing and sales reps for their new "boss".

Aren't these the signs of times?

# 2022

# THE WORD OF THE LORD FOR 2022/5782 AND ONWARD
# "LET THERE BE LIGHT!"

*Given through Apostle Steve Lyston, Pastor Michelle Lyston, Bishop Doris Hutchinson, Prophetess Sophia DiMuccio, Prophetess Nadra Brotherton, Prophet O. Onesta Jolly.*

5782 (or 2022) is the year of the Lord's Release – a year of jubilee, harvest, the year of release. (Leviticus 25: 1 – 7). Great provision will be made for God's faithful ones. It is the year of humanitarian help for the poor and where the Law of Gleaning will be in effect; and those who practice this law will be extraordinarily blessed. Those who are faithful will experience God's blessings and a time of rest. There will be redemption of property and restoration. Many captives will be set free, and there will be debt release, debt forgiveness and debt cancellation. (Deuteronomy 15: 1 – 2). Those companies and organizations who practice the *Shemita* principle will flourish. This is the year of the and great harvest. Those who fail to honor this principle will crash. Many companies and financial institutions will close.

The number 7 will be critical in this season – in the year 2022. For example, Revelation 7, Revelation 17, Daniel 7, Genesis 7 and the 7th book of the Old Testament – Judges. The 7 churches will be important for us watch. Also look at the first 7th plagues and particularly the 7th; namely, the water turned into blood, the plagues of frogs, lice and mice as well as the livestock disease, boils and skin disease, and hail will occur in this Shemita year unless Pharaoh lets God's people go. Pay attention also to the first 7 tribes particularly the tribe of Dan. Dan means "judge; the scales of Justice. Be vigilant in the $7^{th}$ month – July (in the Gregorian Calendar) and Tishrei (in the Jewish Calendar) and the $7^{th}$ of each month.

Remember the 7 lampstands (Exodus 25: 37). Look also at the 7 attributes of God. (Isaiah 11: 2); the 7 Woes. (Matthew 23); 7 parables (Matthew 13); 7 things the Lord hates; 7 letters to the 7 Churches. 70 times 7 which equal the number 490. 7 bowls (Revelation 16: 1; Leviticus 26: 18). The 7 stars in God's right hand. 7 seals and 7 trumpets. (Revelation 1: 4; Revelation 5: 1; Revelation 8: 2) 7 annual Holy Days which carries the 7 benefits of atonement. 7 miracles of God's holy sabbath. The number 7 means completeness, Divine perfection, holy, rest and relates to Genesis 1's Creation. Study about the Shemita.

A new anointing shall God pour out in the world that they will see that He is greater and that His people are greater.

The Lord says some of us are not anointed just for the sake of being anointed, but for a kingly sake. Many of the whites have visited the black race and have taken away their tribes, their gold, their inheritance and their wealth.

The blacks were seeing themselves as slaves when they are kings. The Lord is restoring their kingly status. He is releasing a Breaker Anointing.

A great woe is coming. Those that are leaders are to take care of people. Things have gone to the extreme. Where are the leaders when all these things are happening? This will happen to every human being on the face of the earth. A woe is going to take those whose hearts are like stone. They are going to make some laws like the communist laws. Politicians will make plans that will shock the nations of the world. God is going to show them a sign and only those who serve Him in Spirit and in Truth will stand.

Leaders of the world, you know the anointing and the authority God has given to His people, why are you trying to take away God's people's inheritance again?

2 massive evils are about to be exposed in the world. When this evil is revealed it will cause great suffering to everyone. All Christians and world leaders seek the Lord now!

Remember also the 7$^{th}$ Watch and the 7$^{th}$ hour according to the Jewish time.

There will be liberty and a fresh start for the faithful globally. The market conditions within nations and the financial sectors will experience a whirlwind of issues. All eyes will be on Real Estate, World Currencies and Health.

Up to September 2022, it is critical for God's people to come into His Presence and seek Him to reveal what lies ahead, because the system of Babylon will be falling. (Jeremiah 25: 5 – 6, Jeremiah 27: 12 – 13)

For many who disobey the Lord God, they will find themselves in exile. Many Governmental Administrations globally will crash. Babylon will be conquered and overthrown.
The year 2022 will be a Year of Great Surprises. Humans will stand amazed. Then after a while, that person will disappear. It will cause confusion of the mind. If believers don't pray constantly, many will lose their minds.

Speak the truth! I, the Lord desire of you my people, the truth. And because you will not obey me, I will send destruction among my people. Many people suffer and will lose their eternal home with their creation. Your untruths will come back to haunt you.

Human beings will be so sick, walking up and down searching for help and food. They will be so weak that they stand before you and fall dead. Because of your hard heart and lack of love for my people. Why turn away from my words. You refuse to repent and take heed to my prophetic word spoken by my prophets. Judge not or you will be judged. Take heed of my warnings – no one will be able to help the other. You are going to see things happening in this world that you have never seen or heard of before. Pray for Holland Tunnels and Lincoln Tunnel and all bridges, the Statue of Liberty ambush lies the evil one. Because of the evil things that people will be doing, they will be disguising themselves that they will not be identifiable. The worst is yet to come. This is the time for all those who do not repent to do it now!

Leaders – spiritual and otherwise – are planning to go anywhere they want to go and not be seen. But it will not happen.

More massive disasters are going to hit this world. (Isaiah 21). All idols are going to be destroyed from their secret places. The great spoil is yet to come. I am weary of our doings says the Lord God. If you repent, I will deliver you. The great spoil is about to come upon the earth. It is getting late.

It is time for all believers to pray without ceasing. It is time for all the unsaved to repent and take heed. The slaughter of my sons and daughters are coming to an end. Many countries will experience great loss because of rapid disasters.

5782/2022 will also be a Year of Building – building the tabernacle and the family. It is the year also, of ownership and great faith.

It is the year of completion, as well as judgement upon the wicked who refuse to repent. (Ezekiel 9: 3 – 6). Remember also, that judgement begins in the House of God. (1 Peter 4: 17)

It will be the end of one era and the beginning of a new one.

It is the year of Truth and exposure of corruption globally. The banking sector will experience a crash in certain of its areas. The stock markets will also experience a crash and there will be a major decline in the Real Estate Industry.

It will be an unexplainable year. Many will not be able to explain certain happenings, but those whose foundations are strong in God will stand. Many kingdoms will fall; many leaders will be removed. There will be disaster, chaos in this year 2022/5782.

Watch the stroke of midnight 2021, for this is where many persons will denounce their allegiance for monetary gain worldwide across government bodies, the church, family and businesses. (Watch the 30 pieces of silver) – Great Betrayals ahead! Keep a close watch on your friend-enemies.

The guards assigned to earth form heaven is slated to change in February 2022 and again in August 2022. The world will be tested even more. God is saying to his people, be sure to be hold on tight, be sure to be connected to me. There is a pruning that must take place. Many are set to gain the world and lose their souls. As I sift, some are falling through.

In the Body of Christ, many leaders are no longer interested in doing the will of God. Many will return to the world. God will be transferring their blessings to others who are faithful. The Lord says this is the greatest time in history to evangelize. Also, when God uses someone, that person must see it as a privilege. All who laugh now will be silenced. He will go through any barrier just to bless His people.

Many more churches will fall into apostasy and close. We must also pray consistently for Marriages and family in 2022 and onwards.

# The Jewish Year 5782 And The Prophetic Meaning

Overall, the Jewish year 5782 prophetically means *Ur*, which means **"To awaken, stir up, excite, raise up, arouse to action; arouse oneself, alert."** God is calling the Body of Christ to be alert, vigilant, stirred up and to arise, wake up, inspire, alarm, excite, and light.

5782 will be a year of light and the year of awakening for some. It is the Year of the manifestation of the sons of God in the earth. God will begin to stir up many out of their comfort zone like an eagle would. The eagles will begin to rise and the House of God is about to awaken.

Let us take a look at the meanings of the numbers in the year 5782.

*5* is the letter *Hei* and in Hebrew can mean "*here is, to be disturbed or behold.*"

*7* is the letter *Zayin* and in Hebrew can mean "*crown, weapon or sustain.*"

*8* is the letter *Chet* and in Hebrew means "*life.*"

*2* is the letter *Bet* and in Hebrew means "*house.*"

It is a year of faith, the shaking of idol worshipping and the falling of Babylon as in Genesis 11 with the Tower of Babel. Many systems built without God – built on sand, will fall. It will be judgement on the House of Nimrod. Men will rule but God will overrule. Many systems, decrees and protocols will be overturned. God will scatter them.

God is calling His people out of and away from idol worship. it is time for god's people to "COME OUT FROM AMONG THEM..." His people must come out from the lies, deception and sin! It is time to rise up, come out of the darkness and into the True Light! Everything shall be shaken.

As the world continues to focus on COVID-19, the Body of Christ must prepare and be ready to minister spiritually to doctors and nurses. Many will fall into depression because of the stress and many will get sick after taking the vaccine.

## 2022 – The Year Of Light

As 2022 arrives the word will be **"Let There Be Light!"** It will be the year of Light. There will Be a lamp which will bring clear direction to the remnant.

It will be a year of Divine Authority as God will restore order while exposure takes place. (Psalm 119: 105; Genesis 1: 3)

The Ahab and Jeroboam types of leadership will be removed from the scene.

The Book of Genesis will be critical in 2022, and the following are words on which we must focus for this year.

| | | | |
|---|---|---|---|
| Time | Light | Heaven | Earth |
| Sky | Seas | Sun | Moon |
| Stars | Planets | Land | Plants |
| Fish | Birds | Animals | Man |

God will heal and deliver many families and restore generations. This year, the Body of Christ should focus on the Family.

Furthermore, we will see:

a) The manifestation of the True Light – Jesus Christ – throughout the globe, and the saints should Declare His Glory! (Psalm 96: 2 – 4; John 12: 46; John 3: 21 and Matthew 5: 14 – 16)

b) The globe filled with the knowledge, wisdom, solutions, truth and revelations of God, and many eyes will be opened. The false doctrines, errors, deceptions, and lies will be uprooted.

God will:

a) Deal with the spirits of Haman, Jezebel and Ahab so that the faithful will be promoted. The Book of 3 John is a critical one to read.

b) Bless His faithful physically, spiritually, and financially.

His faithful ones must pay especially keen attention to the terms Light, Daylight, Ignite, Illuminate, Bright, Lamp, Sunny, Shine, Happiness, Joy and Breakthrough.

## Jamaica

1. 2022 marks the year of serious labor pains for not only Jamaica and the USA but all over the world. It will take the grace of God for even the elect to stand. However, a great change is coming forth. While man is planning, God is wiping out. In the midst of a boom for some parts of the economy a turnover will take place.

2. "LAMENTATION WILL TAKE PLACE! WEEP, WAIL AND MOURN!" says the Lord. For the Lord says, "Many church men have joined with Leviathan for help, but there will be no help. Many will soon know how important the Word of God is; some will want to eat and cannot! A massive sign will be show in Jamaica. A major change is coming.

3. Pray for the 7$^{th}$ Prime Minister.

4. Jamaica needs to tread carefully regarding going Republic, as it may cause things to worsen. The nation must be extremely careful as it may bring further enslavement and oppression more intense than the Colonial masters. We should seek the Lord on the direction for Jamaica rather than following suit of other

countries. Fix the constitution to benefit the people of the nation rather than a sect among the people. The country may end up in a constitutional crisis which may further damage the image of the nation. Be warned.

5. The word JUDGEMENT is written in red on top of the government buildings in Jamaica.

6. Major money laundering is taking place. Boxes of money are moving out the country. We must be careful that the nation will not be labeled as a capital for illegal currencies. The cost of living will skyrocket and there will be continuous price increases.

7. The Government of Jamaica made some very grave decisions that will cost them financially, socially and spiritually in 2023. These decisions will gravely affect the health sector and economic sector. Many church leaders and business sector leaders had joined forces with the government for financial gain. This was done at the cost of the lives of the average citizens. Even those that thought they knew what they were getting themselves into are going to be shocked.

8. War will break out in the USA, China and Jamaica. God wants His people to be ready. Many politicians in Jamaica will get the COVID-19 virus unless they repent and turn from the direction they are going. The Lord says, "Too many lies and deception!"

9. There will be more corruption and more contract killings. The Police Force will have their hands full. As

gunmen rise up, policemen will be calling the Reserve. We pray for the entire East Kingston.

10. There is a ring operating in Jamaica's 14 Parishes that have been recruiting and using boys, promising them a lot of money and it has been contributing to the crime and violence in the nation and the Lord says it must stop now! The young people are being destroyed for money.

11. Pray for the following places in Jamaica:

| | |
|---|---|
| Port Royal | Morgan's Harbour |
| Palisadoes Road | Norman Manley International Airport |
| Harbour View | Copacabana (in Bull Bay) |
| Cooper's Hill | Seven Miles (Bull Bay) |
| Graham Heights | Cockburn Pen |
| Pines Boulevard | Birdsucker Lane |
| Up Park Camp | |

12. There will be confusion in the Private and Public Sectors regarding contracts and employment. Constitutional issues will also arise.

13. There will be many trojan horses arriving in the nation for control of the land.

14. Jamaica's Accountant General and Contractor General will have serious disagreements which will bring great exposure. Unless Coney Island remains closed, there will be serious problems ahead.

15. Pray for the following Government Ministries:

>   Education
>   Tourism
>   Finance
>   Health
>   Security

16. As there are serious challenges ahead; as the nation has
    refused to seek God for His Divine Guidance.

17. Jamaica! Jamaica! For survival, look to farming – look
    to God!

18. The communications systems in Jamaica are in trouble. Nothing is safe and no one is safe.

19. Jamaican Travel Service business in trouble and will shut down in some cases. There will be major problems and major changes in the Ministry of Labour in Jamaica.

20. Pray for the following:

>   | | |
>   |---|---|
>   | Sizzla | Shaggy |
>   | Tiger | Jimmy Cliff |
>   | Bounty Killer | Beenie Man |
>   | Sean-Paul | Faye Ellington |
>   | Cliff Hughes | Usain Bolt |

Pray for God's intervention in their lives.

21. We shall see shifting and shaking like never before; every sector shall experience the shifting and the shaking; and strongholds shall come down. We will also see many things shifting worldwide. Statues and temples will be shaken and shall be as a sign to the peoples. Major changes and shaking shall come to the governments of Jamaica, United States, Mozambique and India. The Church in Jamaica must be prepared for what is coming. It will cause great revival in the country. The gospel will be preached throughout the country.

22. In Jamaica there will be a stir within both political parties. The older set will be "pouring the fuel" while the younger set will be "striking the match and starting the fire." The younger ones will begin to rise up and takeover. Many will be saying that they regret certain political decisions they have made over the years.

23. The Lord is urging the Jamaican Government to do urgent assessments and begin to close its borders from some countries, because the country is now facing grave danger regarding viruses. Most of the viruses are coming from the African region.

24. Many things will backfire for the present administration in Jamaica.

25. There is too much pressure on the people of Jamaica.

Tears, pain, oppression, heartbreak due to the loss of a loved ones. While the people mourn, their cry has been ignored; meanwhile they search for more ways to oppress the people. But the Lord says a day is coming. Every man will be judged for their stewardship. Many oppressors will flee from the Land. The oppressors have opened the portal of death on God's people but watch the hands of the Lord.

26. There is a serious plot from the enemy through political and civil groups against the Churches in Jamaica - a serious dragnet has been set in Jamaica. More Pastors/Bishops will sell their Churches and congregation (flocks) to relieve themselves of all burdens to seek material riches.

## International

27. The Lord says to the nations:
28. This is the time, the hour and the very season that God
needs and is expecting the people, especially the Politicians from all nations to bow their hearts and minds totally to Him – showing reverence to Him – the King of Kings and the Lord of Lords. He needs them to understand that no one exists on his own, nor made himself/herself, (Psalm 100: 3), but that each person on this earth was made in the likeness and image of God – The Father, The Son and The Holy Spirit for a purpose and one such is to acknowledge

Jesus Christ as the Son of God, acknowledge their weaknesses, acknowledge that if they continue to do things by might and by power that nothing will stand and that this will only give man and the devil's earthly glory.

29. Man is also to acknowledge that they are nothing without Him, as He has shown from time-to-time since Genesis to Revelation, and to acknowledge that He is the Only Way, The Truth and The Life. He says He needs the Nation Leaders to come out of Rebellion and Pride.

30. There is no way out of the current situation, but by putting the Word of God into action in order to restore what the locusts have already eaten. He says that the nations have executed injustices to the poor, fatherless and the widow, committing high levels of sin without repentance, shutting Jesus Christ out of our affairs and the affairs of our business.

31. The Lord says He is "… dealing with the continuous oppression by the rich and robbing the wages of the laborers who mow your fields, which you kept back by fraud, has caused their tears to fall, their cries have reached up to Me and will not go unavenged! The heavy burdens of taxation upon the poor have also reached up to Me" He says, "…now is the time to address these issues, as nations-in the right way and if not done, cycles will continue to persist."

32. The Lords says there will be great shaking taking place
    at airports globally – both spiritually and naturally! Shaking in governments globally – both spiritually and naturally. Many Jews will take the streets with their shofar and tallit as a revival will begin to break out among them.

33. Pray for the Caribbean as a time of disaster is ahead. The Lord revealed, inundation and dislocation concerning Caribbean islands. Famine, flood, earthquake and typhoon-like disasters ahead.

34. A great purging and cleansing of the Temple will take place. The Anti-Christ will rise (Revelation 17) and so will the Harlot that sits on many waters; many more will be deceived.

35. God wants His people to continue to stockpile various
    vital items as there will be a great shortage of oil, food, and water which will further trigger the famine. God will deal with the black market in 2022.

36. Watch of Russia and China in late 2022 and early 2023. The news coming from these areas will shake the world. Also, the USA will take some bold moves at the in 2023. These plans were always in place, but it will manifest in late 2022.

37. O Canada! Prepare for impact!! We pray for the nation and for the airline industry. Furthermore, a

shaking is coming for many global leaders, especially Canada and France.

38. More disasters will take place globally because of greed
and wealth. The activities being carried out – fracking, interfering with the atmosphere, the sun and the other heavenly bodies will create more earthquakes, flooding, landslides and disasters.

39. We must pray for President Biden, the White House and the entire Washington DC. There is going to be significant in-fighting among the Democrats and many will want the President to go.

40. Pray against a sex scandal repeat in the White House, and for all the US Embassies worldwide and pray against attacks.

41. Something terrible is going to happen to England at Downing Street. There is a cloud hanging over all states in the USA. What is going to happen only prayer can stop it. There is a group that is meeting and planning against the government. Hearts are bitter.

42. A major sweep will take place in New Zealand, Africa,
China, India, North Korea, South Korea, Australia, Russia, Croatia, The Philippines, Finland, Germany, France, Indonesia, Italy, Syria.

43. Pray for the Prime Minister of South Africa. Documents will be revealed which will cause problems among the people.

44. As a result of the interference of the scientific community with the sun, we may see a global heatwave from which many will die. It will also cause famine and bankruptcy. We should watch the months of April to December. But the Lord says if the Church cries out in repentance according to 2 Chronicles 7: 14 water will flow and He will heal the land. There will be drought and lack of water globally. (Zephaniah 2 & 3)

45. A serious "game" of connect-the-dots is taking place hidden in plain site while the global decision-makers put forward decisions at the expense of souls, but the Lord is about to make the next move on their chessboards. Checkmate is coming! Furthermore, the cults and the occult world are abuzz to put plans in place for the children and youth particularly through health, education, technology and music, but do not neglect to keep your eyes on the things that seem simple. Pray for the children and youth like never before.

46. Pray for India as there are serious problems ahead for them. Pray also for Iceland, there are great treasures there. Pray for Pakistan, Bulgaria, Haiti, London, and Ireland as well.

47.   Pray for:

   a. The Vice President of the USA as frustration and undermining increase. She will find out that she was being used. Pray also for her marriage.

   b. The Pentagon as great confusion and betrayals are looming.

   c. The French Prime Minister, and regarding any plans to overthrow him.

   d. Saudi Arabia, especially the crowned prince. A sensitive document will be revealed and get into the wrong hands, which will create problems.

   e. Buckingham Palace as more things will be uprooted and there will be more scandals.

   f. Bill Gates, something is going to take place with him. Pray for his health and salvation.

   g. The US President and the First Lady. Betrayals, betrayals, betrayals, especially by close persons. Pray concerning President Joe Biden's health and spiritual life.

   h. The current political administration in the US that they will make wiser decisions that will please GOD.

i. Pray that all the oppressors of the poor, the fatherless and the widow bow their hearts to the Lord before it's too late.

48. Pray against:

   a. Electrical blackouts in New York and other states which may cause violence to breakout. Brooklyn is in trouble, pray for them. Pray especially for the poor the fatherless and the widow. New York should also make way for a new governor.

   b. Any attempts regarding the Pope.

   c. A tsunami hitting Malawi.

49. Things will come to the point where the various sectors
will be calling the true servants of God to ask them what to do. Hospitals will be calling the Church to come in to pray because of the breaking out of diseases and plagues about to take place.

50. A major exposure will take place concerning China, and regardless of what they try to do to hide it, it will not be covered up. What will be exposed globally will affect them significantly and impact their business with other nations.

51. There are going to be major happenings in the US

territory islands, and it will affect the USA financial and cause crashes throughout the US economy. Many will want to blame the US President, but the problem existed before that President. The problem had been festering for years prior.

52. The USA and other nations should postpone all major
    gatherings and mass holiday celebrations, especially in Manhattan, Times Square and other major sites and venues. (Remember, a leopard doesn't change its spots.)

53. The Real Estate industry in the USA will go through another storm and shaking, but in the midst of that God's people who are faithful will be land possessors again.

54. More Oppressive legislation or going to be past because of the greed of the private sector

55. The Spirit of death has been released over the USA and
    the because of the declaration as well legislations made by leaders at state and federal level and the Church must prayer.

56. The Church must pray that the People of The USA and
    the World will look to God and not man for solution.

57. Abortion is on the rise, but the spirit of the Lord says that He will heal and deliver. We will see the Spirit and the Lord moving upon many who are in agreement with abortion, and their eyes will be opened to the truth.

58. God wants the youths to be aware of the deception and
    destruction of the feminist Movement.

59. Barbados will begin to experience a temporary prosperity because of the direction that they have taken – made the nation a Republic, and has begun to open-up fully to the "Goat Nation". However, because they have been building on sand, there will be a great fall. The government of Barbados and the Church need to seek God – the solid rock and work closely together to genuinely eradicate poverty that has affected the family, the elderly, children everywhere. The severity of poverty has caused different people to do anything to attain money illicitly and immorally. If Barbados does not seek God and turn away from their current direction, their fall will be resounding.

60. There are major surprises ahead for the Banking Industry, and Insurance Companies (health, home, business and car).

61. Many tax audits will be carried out on Politicians, especially regarding their businesses, as well as with huge conglomerates.
62. Many prisoners who were unjustly accused of crimes they did not commit, will get a chance for their truth to be heard and be released.

## Climate Change

63. The constant interference of space by Scientists and billionaires have caused the weather patterns to change and there are more natural disasters approaching the earth, more so because of man's rebellion against God.

64. There will be more delays with flights worldwide because of the drastic change in the weather predicted for a particular week or month, this will be further loss of monies for airlines and passengers.

65. There will be more buildings collapsing because of major flooding in flood-prone and non-flood-prone areas in Bangladesh, Peru, Indonesia, India.

66. For too long, Scientists have interfered with the sea animals for various testing and further depleting them by destroying the Ocean with toxic chemicals, but this is about to come to an end, says God.

67. Major heatwaves are expected for Jamaica, Costa

Rica, Puerto Rico, Panama, Osceola Florida, Mexico, Guatemala, Ecuador, Honduras, Haiti and Trinidad & Tobago.

68. More Meteor Showers are expected because of the damage to the Ozone Layer.

69. The transportation industry will take a plunge because of the upcoming shutdown of the Nations' borders, which will be worse than before.

## Health

70. The Spirit of the Lord says their instruments will not work that have been constantly used to bring harm concerning the COVID-19. There are different notable people who have interfered into the atmosphere causing more people to be sick. There are many different strands that are strategically placed into the atmosphere as a population reducer.

71. No vaccine nor booster shots will be beneficial to anyone. There is going to be a new surge of the coronavirus among those who have already taken the vaccine. Many will regret taking it. There will also be much in-fighting, sabotage and conspiracy among politicians globally. Some will be poisoned.

72. Many animals have been carrying the virus and this will be dangerous for any human beings.

73. Pray for all pilots and airline worker, both commercial
    and private, as many will suffer from COVID-19-related issues and complications, which may endanger both health and security.

74. The US government has plans now to shut down the entire country and other countries worldwide will follow what the United States has done.

75. Unless mandatory vaccines are reversed, there will be:

    - More deaths and more health complications.
    - Significant reduction in travel
    - Reduction in Tourism and significant shortfall for the hotel industry
    - Violations of religious rights
    - Population reduction
    - Emergence of other variants and weakening of
    - the immune system
    - Increase in the number of Mental Health Issues
    - Release of the four (4) Horsemen
    - Devastation of the workforce

76. The Lord now wants His people to cry out for Him to give them a cure. (2 Chronicles 7).

77. Many more nurses and doctors who will be leaving the health industry for every state within the US.

78. The death toll in France, Russia, Syria, Jamaica (The Caribbean, Nigeria, South Africa, Puerto Rico, and Mexico shall increase.

79. There will be great uprisings concerning the vaccines throughout the US and the rest of the world.

80. Scientists, Politicians and other major influential people are responsible for many children who are affected badly as a consequence of the vaccines worldwide. Furthermore, as the disease and viruses increase, they will develop and market more vaccines which will cause things to become worse.

81. The Lord wants the world to prepare for the next plague that will breakout in the form of a skin disease. We need to watch out for the Japanese hornets. They will fly in great groups.

82. My angels are walking the land and taking record. They see the hearts of my people and they are making record of who to save from the pestilence that already has been unleashed on this earth. Stay consecrated. Stay entrusted in me. Stand firm, be watchful, prayerful, do not stand down. Do not leave the wall. Exposure is about to happen and when it does war

will begin. Not world war; civil war is about to break out. You are safe as long as you stay faithful and consecrated.

## Body Of Christ

83. Get ready for reset.

84. In April 2020, the Lord said to give Him 3 years. A reset is on the way. People of God be ready. We do not know when God will come back and we do not know how He intends to reset. Hold on, 2022 will get worse before it gets better. This is the time to start making plans for survival. This is the time to seek God while He can be found. This is not the time to play church. Church leaders who made decisions without the directive of the Holy Spirit will soon understand and meet the consequences of their actions. Woe to the Shepherds that led their flock astray. Woe to those that sold out and listened to the wisdom of men stead of God. Those that trusted in horses and Chariots will fall but those that Trust in God will stand firm.

85. The Body of Christ must first sincerely repent for our sins, turn from our wicked ways and make it right with Him and begin to truly set an example for the world to see. Let the world see Christ – The Hope of Glory! He says, "He will sit as a Refiner and Purifier of silver; He will purify the sons of Levi and purge

them as gold and silver, that they may offer to the Lord an offering in righteousness." "Then will the offering of Judah and Jerusalem be released to the Lord as in the days of old, as in former years." "And I will come near you for judgment; I will be a swift witness against sorcerers, against adulterers, against perjurers, against those who exploit wage earners and widows or orphans, and the alien because they do not fear Me", says the Lord of Hosts." "For I Am the Lord, I do not change; therefore, you are not consumed, O sons of Jacob. Yet from the days of your fathers, you have gone away from My Ordinances and have not kept them." Return to Me and I will return to you," says the Lord of Hosts. But you said, "In what way shall we return?" Israel neglected her relationship (covenant) with God through robbing Him of their tithes and offerings, Israel's neglect brought judgment in the form of retribution, God then challenged Israel to counter their neglect by proving His faithfulness in this matter of giving and challenged them that if they would tithe and give their offering because He would open the windows of Heaven and rebuke the devourer with His Rain. He would destroy the locusts that devour crops.

86. The Spirit of the Lord says we do not truly understand

"His Glory." He says "Who do we think Apostle Paul said that he counts it all joy what he is going through." He says "Apostle Paul had many wonderful experiences in Him and what He experienced in the flesh, did not compare to what he experienced spiritually. The more we go through, the more we shall experience Hi Glory! He says, "His Glory is not cheap, and it does not fall unto man's lap, but one has to go through what I have allowed because I have allotted the Grace to each one of you." "You are going through for My sake, and it is worth it!" "Though the world is going through turmoil, these are the greatest times for My People and the ones who will reap the benefits more are His Faithful Ones!" "This is not the time to give up, but all need to stand in their positions and Fight!"

87. There will be more exposures concerning the "CHURCH" that will cause many to scatter, especially concerning gospel artists – not many are faithful to GOD anymore.

88. Seek the Lord for solution children of God. For there is always a solution. Some of God's children are still thinking within the box and looking for their solutions in the ways of old. There is a new way of life.

89. The word and wisdom of God will seem like foolishness to those that do not truly believe in Him. There will be persecution against His word. However, time will tell; but when the truth shows up, do you want to be caught off guard? I see a large mountain crumbling. I see destruction but with it,

exposure. The Lord wants his people to study and have hope in Revelations 14. The Lord is coming.

90. God is shortening the day for His Elect. Yes, you will see the loss of lives of some of God's people, but to be absent from the body as a child of God is to be present with God. However, there are two sickles that are in rapid operation. These are the sickle of God and the sickle of the Enemy. There is a great reaping taking place. In which vineyard do you belong?

91. We are in the eleventh hour, and so God is calling His people to rise. The anti-Christ is gaining ground because God's people have become lukewarm and have been sleeping. A global shaking is about to take place. Things will never be the same. The usual way of governing will be shaken. (Matthew 20: 6 – 9)

92. God is calling intercessors to rise up, as great shaking is coming; the occult groups are coming together against the Church. Pray for all Five-fold ministries as the enemy wants to target them.

93. There Is a New Prophetic wind Blowing and God is rising New People with this gift.

94. Those who desire to be use must get ready for the

outpouring of the anointing and the gifts of the spirit.

95. God is moving away from the "old prophet" because they have been disobedient and carnal minded.

96. Those that move in the gift of Prophecy must guard your heart from pride and greed. Do not be deceive by those prophets that have been refused by God because greed and carnality.

97. Crime and violence will be on the rise like never before, and the Church must pray. Also pray for the low-income communities

98. Pray for Bishop T.D. Jakes as there will be a lawsuit looming that is to take him down.

## Entertainment & Media

99. God is now calling and all Pastors and Christian leaders in the Black community including the Gospel Entertainers and Artist to repent and turn. A time of great oppression and crying out is looming. A time like never before and Many have been led astray by Christian Leaders that has lost their way.

100. More secular entertainers will convert to Christianity in 2022.

101. More news anchors will be retiring in 2022.

102. Pray against major accidents concerning entertainers (secular and gospel).
103. Pray for Oprah Winfrey that she surrenders to the Lord

   now, and pray also for Mariah Carey and her family.

104. Jeannie Mai and Jeezy (Jay Wayne Jenkins) The Lord

   wants to use you and he wants you to surrender to Him Totally. Also, God desires to expand your family, and He desires that you all be dedicated to the Lord for His work.

105. **Jekalyn Carr** God wants you to start focusing more on

   him again and go deeper in him. He is calling you out from among them and to be separated. Your ministry is more than singing there is more that God requires of you.

106. God has refused a lot of Gospel singers and they now moving under a strong delusion and God will judge them greatly. Now is the time turn and repent that your soul might be same

107. Many of the entertainers' whose eyes will open to the deception of the occult of which they are a part.

108. The Lord is going to rock the music industry hard. He

is giving those who say they represent Him to break away from the puppetry the world has them under. They must ask Him to deliver them from the contracts they have signed and deals they have made which have them bound. He requires the full obedience of those who present themselves as His Levites and worshippers. They have forgotten, even forsaken their first love.

109. Pray for the Latin American Christian music community. The Lord is going to move among them, because there are many who have been misguided into signing agreements and now have regrets – they can't see a way out. Some have engaged in deception having been deceived and even their marriages and families are at risk. The Lord is ready to deliver and use them if they are willing to walk away and come back to His plan for them. The Lord is also going to reveal Himself in a specific way to the Pastors/Shepherds in the Latin American community. Pray for Marcos Yaroide, Laura Cardenes, David Green, Alex Zurdo, Christine D'Clario.

110. Pray also for Cece Winans, Bebe Winans, J. Moss, Karen Clark-Sheard, Richard Smallwood, Yolanda Adams, Byron Cage, Kurt Carr, Tauren Wells, Lecrae, Tasha Cobb-Leonard, Kierra Sheard-Kelly, Tori Kelly. They are each about to have an experience with the Lord that will change everything. Their eyes are about to open to the truth.

*These Prophecies given are for 2021 onward. God can choose to hold His hand back from any form of judgement pending, subject to the repentance of nations and individuals. Jonah 3: 5—10; Exodus 32: 14; Jeremiah 18: 7—11; Amos 7: 3—6; II Kings 20: 1—11 and I Corinthians 13: 9. Please remember, God does whatever He pleases (Psalm 135: 6; Psalm 115: 3). He changes Times and Seasons; He removes kings and raises up kings (Daniel 1: 20—23).*

# HIGH ALERT 2022!
## By Apostle Steve Lyston
## January 20, 2022

Haggai 2: 6 says, *"For thus says the Lord of hosts: 'Once more (it is a little while) I will shake heaven and earth, the sea and dry land;"*.

As we enter 2022, there are many high alert situations brewing. The term "high alert' simply means "to be ready for strong possibility of an attack or something dangerous happening." It is critical for us – God's people and the World – to be on high alert in this time.

Times and Seasons are critical for us to know, and as children of God, we do not operate as the world does. We must depend on the Holy Spirit, who will reveal all things that lie ahead. He will also reveal to us how to prepare and how to make plans.

## Weather Threats

The first high alert situation is the global weather patterns. We will see shifts in the weather systems in various parts of the world. As the weather evolves it almost seems as if the climate itself is fighting back, because of the sinfulness of mankind.

The Book of Genesis outlines how sin not only affects those around us, but also the climate. We have seen experiments that have gone wrong because of scientific "intervention" into our God-given environment.

Instability will begin to take place within the cosmos – as in Psalm 46 – tsunamis, earthquake, volcanic eruptions, floods and landslides. (Read also 2 Chronicles 7: 13-14).

Also, we will see an economic reset will take place, and so this will be a year of release. (Hebrews 12: 27).

As the shaking continues, transformation will take place. God is shaking ad removing the man-made systems, because mankind has become evil. We will see the manifestation of the Glory of God in the earth. Scientists will be baffled as many of the shakings and flooding will take place without prior warning. In fact, it is critical for every person to seek the Lord before traveling from place to place, as they may travel and cannot return, and it may result in loss of life, record insurance payouts, infrastructural damage, budget breaking price increases.

## War/Terrorism

The next high alert situation is War/Terrorism, and intercessors must be on the wall to pray that our security forces will be on high alert as well.

There cannot be any peace without Jesus Christ. Our security will not be effective unless the Lord build the house. (Psalm 127). Many nations excluded God from their security, and many of them are depending solely on man-made devices – Artificial Intelligence (AI) and robots – which cannot protect us. Our help must come from the Lord in 2022. (Psalm 91, Psalm 121) A leopard never changes its spots, so all nations must be on high alert. It is critical that we seek God to help us identify the true enemy and their plans.

**The Health Industry**

The state of the Health Industry is the next high alert situation.

It is funny that many media and social network entities are censoring those who speak about anything to do with health, vaccines and viruses, particularly (but not only) when solutions are forthcoming.

Didn't God create man? Are you saying that God does not know what to do or how to fix what has gone wrong? Why aren't they being blocked themselves; because they are the ones giving inaccurate and unreliable information?

Everybody wants to go back to normal, but at the rate they are going, we may not see normal any time soon. There are many lies and deceptions floating around today.

**Finance and Food**

This next high alert situation is significant. We need to prepare ourselves for the food shortage that will be taking place, and furthermore, the financial and black markets will crash.

## Solutions

- ✓ Look for new opportunities
- ✓ Focus on land, real estate
- ✓ Practice Biblical Principles, including Tithing.
- ✓ Stockpile/Store all necessary basic items
- ✓ Dig wells, purchase seed and begin to focus on farm
- ✓ Watch out for animals that may be spreading the virus
- ✓ Be on the alert for other variants of the coronavirus
- ✓ Avoid crowded areas
- ✓ Pray for all bridges, major transportation systems; all places of interest globally and pray for every plan of the enemy to come to naught.

Be alert.

# GREAT FAITH IN FAMINE 2022
## By Apostle Dr. Steve Lyston
Posted on January 12, 2022

We have entered into 2022, and based on the path that we are on, unless there is global repentance and Divine Intervention, we are going to walk the path of great famine. There are many instances of famine mentioned in history. The famine of 1769, The Bengal Famine, The Irish Famine of 1845, The Famine of China in 1878 were some which cause a great death toll. With the pandemic and bad decisions made by the global leaders, the globe is being pushed on a path of famine. Amos 8: 11 – 12 says, ""Behold, the days are coming," says the Lord God, "That I will send a famine on the land, Not a famine of bread, Nor a thirst for water, But of hearing the words of the Lord. They shall wander from sea to sea, And from north to east; They shall run to and fro, seeking the word of the Lord, But shall not find it."

The Basis of The Famine Famine and drought were two (2) of the punishments God used against His people. The Book of Amos speaks of a new kind of famine – the famine for the Word of God, which brings serious repercussions. Solutions from the Word of the Lord will be very rare. Man has been trying to silence the truth and they will pay the price – they will be plundered. When God is silent (because man refuses to listen), man will try to silence the truth and will pay the consequences. We are now seeing blatant censorship taking place in the media. Scientists are now failing badly because nothing they are trying to do is working. There are different types of famines mentioned in the Bible – disaster, drought, crop failure, locusts and viruses, war and natural calamity, price increases – and all these are already happening. It will take great faith for people to deal with it. While famine alignment and reset spiritually and naturally, and brings change in the earth, it also allows us to move away from Moab. So, while many are trying to prevent migration, the famine ahead will be so severe that there will be increased migration as people seek for survival. People will be going to and fro. That is why, countries who try to close their borders from the poor will be affected severely. The Law of Gleaning (Leviticus 23: 20 – 22) must be practiced if companies and countries are going to stand.

End-Time Happenings Famine also depicts end-time happenings and has to do with government mismanagement and bad policies, wrong economic priorities, and a lack of policies regarding farming. Many companies and nations are focusing on digital currency, bitcoins, the Metaverse, and AI (Artificial Intelligence) among other things. What use will any of this have when people are dying of hunger?

Price increases, lack of employment opportunities, loss of employment, cause famine and lead to malnutrition and the lack of basic needs, and all this is already rampant in our world now. Many also think that over-population is the cause of famine. That is not true and that thought should never be entertained. Lack of proper stewardship by leaders, and political mismanagement are the main reasons for famine.

Renew Your Mind For the faithful ones, in order to deal with famine their minds must be renewed. We must look to God as our Source; and look to Him for our increase, just as was done with the 5 loaves and 2 fishes. We must also look to receive blessings from unknown places and unknown people. In 2 Kings 4: 38 – 44, there was a man from Baal Shalisha, who came to bless him. It was a place where they worshipped other gods not the True and Living God; and he came to bless the prophet of God. God always blesses His people from the "muddy places". We have to follow instruction and be satisfied with God's provision that He has made for His people. We MUST live by the Word to get wealth – the undiluted word, not false prosperity. We must be led by the Holy Spirit to bring us

through, that we can deal with the problems ahead. In addition to this, the type of doctrine we embrace is critical to our survival. It is also critical for certain nations to remove certain taxes and regulations from certain basic items. Nations must stockpile food and medication now. Any country that has food will have power. Serious contingency plans must be put in place for the poor.

The Just must live by faith!

# FALSE PROPHETS VS. TRUE PROPHETS
By Apostle Steve Lyston
January 13, 2022

From time to time there are those in society who are quick to discredit any true prophetic word given. They deem those who speak as true oracles of God as False Prophets.

Through the years I have come to realize that not many who say such things truly know, nor do they discern who really is a false prophet. Discernment of Spirits is one of the gifts of the Holy Spirit; but then most don't believe in the Holy Spirit nor the gifts of the Holy Spirit. So then, how will they be able to know whether one is false or true. So, each time they hear the true Word of the Lord, they ridicule it.

The Spirit of Mammon is one of the main spirits that influences that kind of response to the prophetic utterances from the Lord. Those under this influence have a form of godliness but deny the power thereof. They compromise and are already fallen away in apostasy.

## Who Is A False Prophet?

There is a difference between False Prophecy and a False Prophet. Many think of a prophet who speaks a word that does not come to pass as a false prophet. But not so.

A Prophet is one of the Ascension Gifts (Ephesians 4: 11). The gift of Prophecy is one of the gifts of the Holy Spirit. (1

Corinthians 12). In explaining to us what a false prophet is, Jesus said to us in Matthew 7: 15 – 20, that it is by their fruits that we shall know them. Galatians 5: 19, tells us that false prophets walk in the works of the flesh. They profess Christianity, but are instead agents of Satan, because as they declare to serve Jesus Christ, they:

i. operate in open sin
ii. engage in witchcraft and the occult (including secret societies);
iii. pull people unto themselves as they touch God's glory.
iv. deny that Jesus came in the flesh,
v. deny that Jesus came by way of the virgin birth.

They can be anybody – a scientist, a doctor, a media personnel, a pastor, a politician, business owner. In the book of Acts, the Apostle Paul declared judgement on Elymas Bar-Jesus, who was an advisor to the Deputy Leader (proconsul). He was a sorcerer, and a false prophet under the disguise of being a man of God; advising the second in command to the nation. How many politicians and "bigwigs" in the nation being advised by false prophets. Acts 8 also shows us that there was a man who was called a mighty man of God, had bewitched an entire city. (Acts 8).

A False Prophet also prophesies for money, accolades, and fame. They will say "It is Peace" when destruction is coming. They are also on the payroll of Jezebel and Ahab. Read Jeremiah 23: 17; Jeremiah 28: 2; Jeremiah 29: 21; 1 Kings 18: 19 – 20; 1 Kings 22: 10 – 12; 2 Peter 2: 15 – 16; and Micah 3: 11 which says "Her heads judge for a bribe,

Her priests teach for pay, And her prophets divine for money. Yet they lean on the Lord, and say, "Is not the Lord among us? No harm can come upon us."

Since the start of the COVID-19 Pandemic, many false prophets of different professions have risen up (Matthew 24: 11 and 24).

We must understand that giving an accurate word and moving in the realm of signs and wonders, does not qualify the person as a True Prophet. (Acts 16).

## Recognizing True Prophets

Every true prophet will be called a false prophet. Jesus, Jeremiah, Ezekiel and Micaiah are examples of such. Jesus was called Beelzebub by the Pharisees and Sadducees. So, test the spirits (1 John 4: 1). Also:

i. Check the fruits with which they function, and check to see if God is getting the Glory from their lives.

ii. Check their lifestyle. True prophets bring the message according to the Word of God. Their messages are always in agreement with God's Word (the Bible). They carry the fruit of the Spirit according to Galatians 5. (Read also Matthew 7: 15 – 20)

iii. True Prophets point people to Jesus Christ, and they do not touch His glory – they lift Him up.

iv. The true prophets carry a burden for the nation.

v. True Prophets do not "eat at Jezebel's table"; they are not her paid puppets.

vi. True Prophets are called by God and are consecrated unto God – set apart; they live right, fear God, walk holy and do not compromise on the principles of God.

So, it is critical to listen to the message of a true prophet, and don't focus on the messenger, as God can use even a donkey to preach His gospel. (Numbers 22: 28). If nations don't repent, even the stones are going to talk; the elements are going to talk.

That being said, the time has come for us to discern, understand and listen to the right voices.

# RUSSIA, UKRAINE AND WHAT IS AT STAKE
by Apostle Dr. Steve Lyston
Posted on March 19, 2022

The current conflict between Russian and Ukraine has opened the door for many things to happen. First of all it is not surprising as this is the Shemita year; this is the year that there will be a shaking of empires.

## The Fight For Superpower Status

The division between the Democrats and the Republicans in the USA has leveled the playing field, and many Western nations now have the opportunity to become the global leader of the West. These nations also have the ambition to become the most militarily dominant nation. They also want to replace the US Dollar and become a global economic superpower – Russia, China and many others are at the top of the heap.

Americans have spent a great deal of time trying to destroy each other from within. America has trampled on the grace God has given them to be the Superpower they have become; however, they have been infiltrated by the Babylonians. They have adopted the Babylonian lifestyle and have exchanged God for Ba'al. If American is to remain on top, then it is critical for them to rebuild the broken altars. They must repent for abortion, racism, classism, and every other kind of prejudice and division in which the people of the nation have been engaged into date.

# The Bear and The Dragon

While Russia and China are uniting to compete against America, it is critical for one to understand that a Bear and a Dragon cannot dwell together. While the Bear and the Dragon compete against the Eagle for the spoils and the resources, there is also a major underlying fight to change political and psychological ideologies at the same time.

If you take a good look at what is happening these days, you will see evidence of socialism dressed as capitalism taking the forefront. There is also a plan to weaken the Trans-Atlantic Partnership.

## Ideological Changes

Both the Bear and the Dragon have capitalist economies, but a communist/socialist leadership structure. There are many who believe that the West has too much democracy. What this means for us, is that the threats against Christianity will not only increase but may even be put into action. So, the Anti-Christ system will expand with a view to eradicating Christianity. Within Socialism, there is only the Marxist ideology, which means that God has no place in any aspect of society and religious freedoms and liberty would be at stake. So simply put, the God of the Universe is on trial. Christians must now engage in serious Spiritual Warfare. We must recognize that the pandemic was all about changing our ideologies – a test to see if we were in the position we need to be, in order to allow them to execute their "ideological makeover", and now the war is about cementing that process.

## Bondage and Famine

The Western Leaders have been blindfolded for years. Many of these leaders have thought that they could operate from two different platforms. They must return to God, or else the Babylonian system will put us in bondage and consume them in the process.

Needless to say, it is critical therefore, for God's people to discern the difference between a snake, a cat, a lion, a dragon, a bear, an eagle and a wolf.

If we take a good look, in the height of the pandemic and the war, laws are being passed to remove some of the ancient landmarks as well as other laws that are the foundation of freedoms, and that is why, if we in the West are to survive, we must return to the Lord.

Further to this, the soaring oil prices, skyrocketing food prices as well as the high cost of living, will send many nations into famine.

## Pledging Allegiance

It is all about pledging allegiance.

There are benefits offered by both Christ and the Anti-Christ. Whatever choice is made will determine the direction of a nation – whether bondage or liberty. While many allegiances are now being formed, it is critical that people select the right allegiance, because everything else is temporary.

There are reasons for every war, and they come with advantages and disadvantages. For example, some wars are to take over the resources of nations. The disadvantage here is that other enemies to the nation create confusion and more deception to awake sleeping giants that have not gone into war with other nations for a while. So attention will be on, Germany, Japan, China, and Iran, but the target may be on the USA and Israel, based on Biblical Prophecies.

The possible advantage is that Christians have the opportunity to join together to win the lost for Christ. Also, there can be dominion and wealth transfer to the Kingdom, because of the suffering they had endured during the pandemic.

We must pray against any nuclear strike based on Zechariah 14: 12 – 15, and that God will give the Body of Christ more time to set its house in order. We pray that this war does not lead us into World War 3 and fulfill the prophecy of Ezekiel 38.

# THE WORD, THE ANOINTING AND THE PROPHETIC
By Apostle Steve Lyston
March 30, 2022

## Old Prophet, Young Prophet

Oftentimes there are Scriptures that are popular but often misunderstood. One such Scripture is 1 Kings 13 – Young Prophet, Old Prophet. Those who are immature or misinformed tend to quickly turn to this Scripture when they don't want to submit and are walking in disobedience. They often try to use this Scripture in the context of age citing that they are the young ones that the Lord is working with now and so they don't have to obey those before them including their shepherd. In no respect was this Scripture speaking about age or seniority.

In this Scripture – 1 Kings 13 – the Lord was speaking about the lifestyle of a prophet, and it meant that an 'old prophet' was one who was stuck in the old ways – and one who has fallen into apostasy; one who compromised the word of God for material and other gain. It meant that an old prophet was one who had gone back to their old lifestyle and was no longer walking in truth. It also meant that they were no longer walking in the fruit of the spirit but were instead walking in the flesh. Thus, that prophet backslid but still functioned in his/her authority like Balaam, and those who were on Jezebel's payroll.

The 'young prophet' referred to one who walked in truth, holiness and righteousness regardless of the cost. They had a holy lifestyle nor tell people what they wanted to hear. Micaiah (1 Kings 22) is one example of the Young Prophet and so is Jeremiah.

So, it is possible to be young in the faith and even young in age and still be an Old Prophet if your lifestyle does not line up with the Word of God. Whenever a person is not walking in the truth, God refers to them as old, and we must always remain Young! This is why as Christians, we can't mix or fellowship with other Christians who are not walking in the truth or holiness. The word even says we are not even supposed to eat (network or affiliate) with them. (1 Corinthians 5)

**Prostitution of the Anointing**

There are many within the Body of Christ, because of their Laziness to seek God, are creating an atmosphere for the prostitution of the anointing. As a result, many prophets are now falling away because of the demands placed on them. Likewise, many churches are going through great financial problems because of a lack of faith. So they have opened a door, and are now creating a monster called Prostitution.

Every prophet's message, maturity and morality are some of the keys we must use to help us discern them. Likewise, they must have the DNA of Jesus in them; and those within the Office of a Prophet must not fall to the temptation and become a Psychic to God's people particularly when they have no intention to read God's Word.

Many of the Pastors need to repent and stop promoting this behavior as it brings reproach to Christ's Church and to Him. Some of them are guiltier than those in the office of the Prophet.

Because of the great reproach upon the Prophetic Ministry, many are now migrating to the office of the Apostle. But before they consider doing so, or taking on a false grace, they better study about the life of an Apostle. It is a life of suffering! The have to become last so that others can be first! I Corinthians 4: 9 says:
"For I think that God has displayed us, the apostles, last, as men condemned to death; for we have been made a spectacle to the world, both to angels and to men."

(Read also I Corinthians 9)


## What Does It Mean: "Favor", "Called", "Chosen"

Many time people will say they are walking in favor; but favor is something that one has to maintain true obedience (Deuteronomy 28: 1 – 14) True obedience and genuine submission to Godly authority. (Luke 2: 49 – 52). Hence, favor – like faith – has a measure. It increases as we continue to walk in God's perfect will. Favor also has to do with those to whom you submit and those you serve. For example, Ruth and Naomi, Elisha and Elijah, Jacob and Laban. Last year's favor cannot deal with this year's issues

So when a person continually walks in disobedience, then that grace and favor will cease to exist and then you will get a true revelation of what favor is all about.

Many times, people say that they are called and chosen by God, but remember that the word says that many are called and few are chosen. So, to be chosen, a person must be able to pass the tests in the timing of God. Of the 32,000 that were called, less than 1% passed the tests; and these tests were simple instructions and required attention to detail and vigilance as well as focus on the kingdom. There must be a steadfast focus on the Kingdom!

So, while many say that they are called and chosen and can't even submit to the leadership of a good mentor, they need to think again. Would the Lord give authority to the ones who won't don't or refuse to submit to authority?

God's criteria for using someone within the Kingdom to carry out His will and purpose is higher and He will not change His word to fit into our desire rather than His will.

# The Word Of The Lord
# April 2022

*The Word of the Lord for the 1st Quarter through Apostle Dr. Steve Lyston, Bishop Dr. Doris Hutchinson, Prophetess Sophia DiMuccio.*

1. I am the God of the universe. Nothing is hidden from me. Watch the first 6 months of this year 2022. It will be a year of mixture – good and evil.

2. The Lord showed a massive boulder coming from nowhere. It rolled through places and destroyed lives, properties, animals and left a trail of suffering behind. Scientists could not determine where it came from. It is a sign. This is a year of many signs and wonders.

3. This is a year for every human being to look up to God.

4. Psalm 93: 1 – 5 – God's faithful ones will receive healing and blessing. Psalm 94: 1 – 23.

5. My people, as you serve me in holiness and truthfulness you will experience my abundant blessings, and you will be able to help the poor and needy who cry out to me day and night.

6. 6 Government ministers are in trouble in Jamaica; and it will soon be revealed.

7. More schools are in trouble in Jamaica.

8. Says the Lord, "You rich and powerful cannot hide from God! Come forth and repent of your deeds! I have seen them all! You allow evil ones to seduce you into the things you know are wrong. Cry out to Me – God, and repent and I will forgive you; or I will remove your candlestick! Stop what you are doing before it is too late!

9. This is the year God is stripping them – the wealthy. They are going to know what it feels like to have nothing. When it happens do not be surprised. At this very moment, their bank accounts are being cleared out. Many of them are used to going to the Lord & Taylor stores to purchase, but many of their cards will decline. Fires will burn their assets. Many will experience the burning bush.

10. The Lord says He is God and His power will be known. This is the year He will be glorified. They have come up with different plans to keep the country in captivity. This is the year to stand up against the forces of darkness.

11. This is the year the media shall be plundered. The Lord says His hand is on the 5-sided stronghold – destruction is coming.

12. China, Russia, Switzerland, Britain, New Zealand – businesses will be going down.

13. Pray against a nuclear strike. Pray for Serbia.

14. The sea is rising and there will be great tsunamis in many countries which will cause a great death toll unless nations repent. They also need to relocate people from living close to the ocean. Pray for Yemen, Pakistan, Egypt, Jamaica, China, Barbados, Dominica. The Lord is waking up the nations.

15. God will show a great sign in Jamaica to the leaders. Also, I saw the sea in Jamaica and the water started stirring with a rage and the waves rose into the air. I also saw the name Germany written in red on a white background. God's fire burned up the paper from the middle and then all around and it was no more.

16. A major famine will hit the globe, and many of the livestock – cows, horses and other animals – will die. Some will die of diseases. Nations will need to store vaccines to combat possible pandemic among the livestock.

17. A political shift will also take place in Jamaica; more challenges ahead.

18. Watch – a female will rise from St. Ann.

19. More private planes will crash globally. This is a

result of sabotage. Pray for all the entertainers, reality show hosts including RF, KK, BKC.

20. Pray against the assassination of 6 world leaders.

**THE WORD OF THE LORD**
by Apostle Dr. Steve Lyston
Posted on May 1, 2022

*Up to April 2022 The Word of the Lord for the 1st Quarter through Apostle Dr. Steve Lyston, Bishop Dr. Doris Hutchinson, Prophetess Sophia DiMuccio.*

I am the God of the universe. Nothing is hidden from me. Watch the first 6 months of this year 2022. It will be a year of mixture – good and evil.

The Lord showed a massive boulder coming from nowhere. It rolled through places and destroyed lives, properties, animals and left a trail of suffering behind. Scientists could not determine where it came from. It is a sign. This is a year of many signs and wonders. This is a year for every human being to look up to God.

Psalm 93: 1 – 5 – God's faithful ones will receive healing and blessing.
Psalm 94: 1 – 23.

My people, as you serve me in holiness and truthfulness you will experience my abundant blessings, and you will be able to help the poor and needy who cry out to me day and night.

6 Government ministers are in trouble in Jamaica; and it will soon be revealed.

More schools are in trouble in Jamaica.

Says the Lord, "You rich and powerful cannot hide from God! Come forth and repent of your deeds! I have seen them all! You allow evil ones to seduce you into the things you know are wrong. Cry out to Me – God, and repent and I will forgive you; or I will remove your candlestick! Stop what you are doing before it is too late!

This is the year God is stripping them – the wealthy. They are going to know what it feels like to have nothing. When it happens do not be surprised. At this very moment, their bank accounts are being cleared out. Many of them are used to going to the Lord & Taylor stores to purchase, but many of their cards will decline. Fires will burn their assets. Many will experience the burning bush.

The Lord says He is God and His power will be known. This is the year He will be glorified. They have come up with different plans to keep the country in captivity. This is the year to stand up against the forces of darkness.

This is the year the media shall be plundered. The Lord says His hand is on the 5-sided stronghold – destruction is coming.

China, Russia, Switzerland, Britain, New Zealand – businesses will be going down.

Pray against a nuclear strike. Pray for Serbia.

The sea is rising and there will be great tsunamis in many countries which will cause a great death toll unless nations repent. They also need to relocate people from living close to the ocean. Pray for Yemen, Pakistan, Egypt, Jamaica, China, Barbados, Dominica. The Lord is waking up the nations.

God will show a great sign in Jamaica to the leaders. Also, I saw the sea in Jamaica and the water started stirring with a rage and the waves rose into the air. I also saw the name Germany written in red on a white background. God's fire burned up the paper from the middle and then all around and it was no more.

A major famine will hit the globe, and many of the livestock – cows, horses and other animals – will die. Some will die of diseases. Nations will need to store vaccines to combat possible pandemic among the livestock.

A political shift will also take place in Jamaica; more challenges ahead.

Watch – a female will rise from St. Ann.

More private planes will crash globally. This is a result of sabotage.

Pray for all the entertainers, reality show hosts including RF, KK, BKC.

Pray against the assassination of 6 world leaders.

## May 10, 2022

The Lord says some parts of Yemen and Australia will be cut off. Let God arise and His enemies be scattered.

The Spirit of ingratitude has risen up. They are no longer seeing Him as God anymore, they are seeing Him as a vagabond. Remind them, if they are ashamed of Him, He will be ashamed of them

# MURDERER, BLOOD IS ON YOUR SHOULDERS
by Apostle Dr. Steve Lyston
June 2, 2022

Proverbs 6: 16-17 reminds us, "These six things the Lord hates,

Yes, seven are an abomination to Him: A proud look, lying tongue,

Hands that shed innocent blood,"

This Scripture says it all. The world continues to break out in disease, disaster, destruction, and in the midst of all that, the shedding of innocent blood continues, and the blood cries out from the earth.

The shedding of innocent blood is taking place for many reasons.

Greed and the lust for wealth and power.
Blood sacrifice and the occult
Envy and Jealousy.
These are some of the main reasons.

When disaster hits a nation, oftentimes the number one cause is the shedding of innocent blood. What many don't understand is that blood has a voice and when it is shed it cries to God for justice. That being said, when a child is aborted, those who are advocates for abortion in this nation and all those involved in the process have blood on their hands. If you kill them outside or inside the womb, you are still a murderer and blood is on your hands.

Many talk about legalizing abortion to prevent what we call unsafe abortions; but there is no such thing as a safe abortion – they are all unsafe and they need to stop the lies. So if you throw a live child in a garbage bin, or take their lives while in the womb, what is the difference?

Leviticus 17: 11, "For the life of the flesh is in the blood, and I have given it to you upon the altar to make atonement for your souls; for it is the blood that makes atonement for the soul." (See also Genesis 4: 10 – 11)

When the One Who gives life hears the cry of the innocent blood, there are curses released upon those who shed the blood and they become vagabonds and fugitives. Furthermore, even the farming community becomes affected because the earth is affected. The scripture says that the earth no longer yields the way it should.

**The Spirit of a Vagabond**

A vagabond is someone who wanders from place to place without a home or a job – they have no settled home. This is the same spirit that affects people who have no settled church home – who wander from church to church. The same is true of those who can't keep a job. The word fugitive also carries a similar meaning.

We often see people suffering greatly financially, emotionally or otherwise and the Lord revealed that the root cause of it will be the shedding of innocent blood. Abortion is also one of those things that fall under that category. So, when one sheds innocent blood there are legal portals open for many problems – sickness, poverty and such things. Did you know that what is now called climate change, is the result of the shedding of innocent blood?

## Climate Change

Leviticus 18 outlines to us that many issues will bring defilement to the earth and different categories of sin as well. Defilement of the earth cause defilement, which will bring a cleansing including earthquakes on the earth and under the sea – tsunamis, tidal waves, volcanic eruption. In the Book of 2 Kings, we see that barrenness was upon the land and the water was bad. So, the prophet of God had to bring healing to the land and ultimately to the city; because there was a cycle and it had to be broken in order for the city to experience true prosperity.

Unless there is global repentance, and major cleansing of the bloodshed, we are going to see a lot of disasters take place over the next 6 months onward.
It does not matter how bloodshed was carried out, nor does it matter who was behind nor who pulled the trigger, nor does it matter if we pass laws to kill the unborn, nor the level of witchcraft involved, nor through deliberate medical acts, nor activities to control population – all involved have blood on their hands.

## Failing To Warn Against Sin

There are many within the Body of Christ, and in particular, in the Fivefold Ministry, those whom God has given the gifts to speak against sin, and to warn the city. Ezekiel 3: 18 says "When I say to the wicked, 'You shall surely die,' and you give him no warning, nor speak to warn the wicked from his wicked way, to save his life, that same wicked man shall die in his iniquity; but his blood I will require at your hand." (See also Ezekiel 33: 8) So, blood is also on the hands of those who God has given the charge to warn of the shedding of innocent blood but instead compromise.

# SEASON OF PENTECOST AND PROPHECIES
by Apostle Dr. Steve Lyston
June 9, 2022

We are in the season of Pentecost, and Pentecost is one of the greatest seasons for mankind. It is the seasons within which the Church was birthed; and it is about ordinary people being empowered to do extraordinary things. It is a time during which God pours out upon his people.

As we read the book of Acts, we see the manifestation of the power of the Holy Spirit. After Passover, God instructed Israel to number 7 Sabbaths plus 1 day, which worked out to be 49 days plus 1 day which in total is 50 days. The number 50 signifies jubilee, liberty/freedom, and is the number for the Holy Spirit. (Leviticus 25: 10). Now it is important for us to realize that we can do nothing without the Holy Spirit. He is God. If Jesus did not carry out His ministry without the Holy Spirit, what say we as a Church. We need the Holy Spirit of God!

Acts 1: 8 says, "But you shall receive power when the Holy Spirit has come upon you; and you shall be witnesses to Me in Jerusalem, and in all Judea and Samaria, and to the end of the earth."

If the Church is going to walk in the Spirit of Excellence, and display God's Divine power, it is critical for us to get back to the Holy Spirit. Many have locked Him out of the Church, while focusing on the world and what it has to offer. A world without the Holy Spirit is just simply chaos and darkness. We have seen both secular and religious leaders fail badly because they have exchanged the Holy Spirit for other spirits; hence the current global problems we now face.

The Holy Spirit is now pouring out His power and His Spirit upon all those who welcome Him.

There are many benefits we receive at Pentecost – Power, Promotion, Purpose and Provision. It is an Upper Room moment of Prayer

**Prophecies**

For the next 6 months, we need to watch global economies. There will indeed be great shaking of the governments and the Church. Meanwhile, the levels of sin and evil will continue to rise, but the Power of the Holy Spirit will increase and intensify. We will also see natural and spiritual earthquakes taking place.

God is calling His people to rise and tear down the strongholds and evils over and within nations. He is also calling the Mothers of Zion to be revived, arise, be refreshed, be empowered and get back on the wall.

Global expansion of the Kingdom will be taking place. A time of refreshing, rebirthing, and renewal. New wine will be poured from the heavens upon the nations and even more so upon His people.

The Lord says we are to pray and watch France and India. He further said that many of the politicians will be removed from the scene that several of them will be arrested at the airport. There are going to be major explosions taking place in Space.

The Lord also says that there will be a massacre taking place in Jamaica. There will be major investigations among billionaires, and many offices will be raided. Many government offices locally and globally will be raided by Law Enforcement.

There will be major division among politicians and government officials which will lead to great exposure. Some politicians' eyes will be opened but it will be too late – particularly concerning contracts they have signed. There will be a changing of the guard soon – from the top to the bottom. However, it is critical for the globe to pray that there won't be missile attacks on the West. A dying bear is dangerous because they will lash out and they have nothing to lose. The West needs to be warned and be on high alert against attacks.

Many are complaining about the shooting currently taking place in the USA, but the root is being ignored. The root cause is sin. The focus should not only be on the one who pulls the trigger, but on who is behind the trigger-puller.
While they lament about school shootings and gun control, there is major neglect regarding the killing of the unborn child, and while I condone neither, we must give attention to both equally.

The Lord is asking the question – "Who will stand up for the voiceless?"

More schools and campuses will close because of shootings. We are about to witness the 4 horsemen according to the book of Revelation. We will now see the pale horse and black horse in effect. The Pale Horse signifies death, disease, water problems, and hunger. The Black Horse signifies food shortages, war, high food prices, scarcity and economic disruption.

There will be a major split within the current political party in government – the like of which has never been seen before. The civilians will begin to express their frustrations and declare that they have had enough.

Hospitals in Jamaica need urgent attention as more supplies will be needed to deal with what lies ahead. They also need more health centers and hospitals within the country. No one should be turned back. Pray for the hospitals.

The Lord says there is a massive wind blowing away the things that are evil.

Many commercial airlines will be grounded, and numerous flight cancellations will occur because of what is going on in the atmosphere. The Lord says He is allowing this to protect His people.

The bear has plans to send missiles to the USA.

There are different terrorist attacks that are staged by popular people.

The Lord says there needs to be health discounts for the people.

The Lord also revealed many caskets lined up side by side.

In Jamaica, many buildings will be shaken down including old church buildings.

# SIN AND GLOBAL DESTRUCTION
By Apostle Steve Lyston
June 25, 2022.

Sin has continued to change the landscape of the environment. The negative effects of climate change is the result of sin. It has caused many to flee their state and nation - New York, New Jersey, and California to name a few. There will be an increasing exodus from different cities, countries and states as a result of the sinful lifestyles.

What lawmakers need to know, particularly those legislate sin and sinful lifestyles, is that sin pays a wage. When you sin, it is work done and you will surely be paid. Sin is a slave-master which demands one to be faithful and committed. All sins matter, so, when you sin, you become a slave to sin and your employer is Satan himself.

**Sin Destroys The Economy**

Sin affects the economy, brings crime and violence and brings disaster. Many are trying to bring solutions while ignoring the main cause of the problem. Matthew 7: 24 – 27 shows us that many are building with sin, but the reward will be bankruptcy and recession, and there will be a great fall unless they build on the rock.

If we want to see an end to viruses and plagues, then we must address the things that are considered to be sin in God's eyes. So many nations are using sin as a cure for sinful activities. We must remember Romans 6: 23. Debt to the cities and nations mean death to your economy, increased debt to the nations and death as well. Ultimately, sin removes the Grace and favor of God from a nation. It also downgrades a nation's economic rating. Furthermore, it brings poverty and curses.

It is critical that even heads of nations and organizations, other businesses, churches and lifestyle all impact operations and negatively impacts productivity.

## Sin – The Separator

Sin separates the individual from God and it also impacts the animals and their habitat. The sin of man even affects the ground by way of curses – barrenness. We are now seeing Agriculture being seriously and negatively affected pushing us to the verge of famine. Many will die of hunger, unless we change our lifestyle.

Romans 8: 20 – 22 says, "For the creation was subjected to futility, not willingly, but because of Him who subjected it in hope; because the creation itself also will be delivered from the bondage of corruption into the glorious liberty of the children of God. For we know that the whole creation groans and labors with birth pangs together until now."

This Scripture reveals to us that there is a connection between the earth and our actions. Many who call themselves experts need to realize that it is man's actions that propel climate change. Until that is understood then a great deal of time will be wasted in meetings going in circles. It is as a result of sin why man now has to labor for what God had planned to extend freely to mankind. Sin caused man to make the wrong choices and birthed greed, corruption, and selfishness – among other things.

## Sin Is Contagious

Sin is contagious. It is time for us to engage in social distancing from sin. Jesus paid the price to cleans us from sin. The only sin that is not forgiven is blasphemy against the Holy Spirit. Remember that sin is a reproach to any nation and that it is righteousness, that will exalt the nation. No nation can be great without righteousness. The way the world treats the poor is a sin and is now impacting the globe negatively. Look at the fact that the air we were freely given by God, and to which we had free access in all places, we now have restricted access and in some cases a violation of our freedom having to wear masks wherever we go; not to mention the monitoring devices that many are being required to wear.

## Breaking Spiritual Laws

The breaking of Spiritual Laws brings serious consequences. If man was taking spiritual laws seriously, then we would have avoided much of the problems we are now facing in the world.

It is surprising to see that many are now rising to power by promising sin as a solution. The sinful heart of man does not have mercy even for the unborn. It is time for us to change our sinful lifestyle so that we an have peace and economic prosperity.

# AMERICA! MAKE JULY 4TH A TIME OF REPENTANCE
by Apostle Dr. Steve Lyston
June 29, 2022

In the time of Gideon (in the Book of Judges), Israel did evil in the sight of the Lord continually, and there was no king in Israel, everyone did what was right in his own eyes, and deliberately served foreign gods. The people broke their covenant with the Lord, and as a result, the Lord delivered them in to the hands of various oppressors. So, each time they cried out to Him, then He would faithfully, send a Judge to deliver the nation – whether civil or military leader – to bring the people back to God in repentance; and to re-establish the broken covenant.

This scenario is comparable to the state America today.

## America Needs A Gideon

Let's take a look at the current picture.

*Homelessness*

Today, America has opened the door for the Midianites of today, to plunder the nation and its resources, bringing impoverishment upon the people of the nation. According to reports as late as March 5, 2022, the number of homeless in the US is estimated at 552,830 and rising. This number does not include persons living in their vehicles.

*Hunger (Food Insecurity)*

According to reports from the USDA (United States Department of Agriculture) According to the USDA, more than 38 million people, including 12 million children, in the United States are food insecure. The pandemic has increased food insecurity among families with children and communities of color, who already faced hunger at much higher rates before the pandemic.

*Recorded Disasters*

In 2021, there were 20 weather/climate disaster events with losses exceeding $1 billion each to affect the United States. These events included 1 drought event, 2 flooding events, 11 severe storm events, 4 tropical cyclone events, 1 wildfire event, and 1 winter storm event. Overall, these events resulted in the deaths of 724 people and had significant economic effects on the areas impacted.

*Mass Shootings*

According to the Washington Post, there have been over 250 mass shootings so far in 2022.

*Abortion*

The CDC (Center for Disease Control) reported that up to 2019, there wer 629,898 legal abortions in 2019. That does not include those unreported or deemed "illegal".

Furthermore, when a nation begins to riot in order to make abortions legal, the nation is walking on a tightrope without a net.

In addition to all this, the US Dollar is losing its power globally and 7 major countries are considering abandoning the US Dollar.

We are seeing disasters of every kind now hitting the nation and all these happenings are signs that the grace and favor that made America great once is now slipping.

While they lament about school shootings and gun control, there is major neglect regarding the killing of the unborn child, and while I condone neither, we must give attention to both equally.

The Lord is asking the question – "Who will stand up for the voiceless?"

More schools and campuses will close down because of shootings.

We are about to witness the 4 horsemen according to the book of Revelation. We will see now the pale horse and black horse in effect. The Pale Horse signifies death, disease, water problems, and hunger. The Black Horse signifies food shortages, war, high food prices, scarcity and economic disruption.

There will be a major split within the current political party in government – the like of which has never been seen before. The civilians will begin to express their frustrations and declare that they have had enough.

Hospitals in Jamaica need urgent attention as more supplies will be needed to deal with what lies ahead. They also need more health centers and hospitals within the country. No one should be turned back. Pray for the hospitals.

The Lord says there is a massive wind blowing away the things that are evil.

Many commercial airlines will be grounded and numerous flight cancellations will occur because of what is going on in the atmosphere. The Lord says He is allowing this to protect His people.

The bear has plans to send missiles to the USA.

There are different terrorist attacks that are staged by popular people.

The Lord says there needs to be health discounts for the people.

The Lord also revealed many caskets lined side by side.

In Jamaica, many buildings will be shaken down including old church buildings.

# THE ALMOND TREE AND THE BOILING POT
by Apostle Dr. Steve Lyston
March 19, 2022

Understanding symbols in the end-time are critical. Jeremiah 1: 11 – 13 tells us:

*"Moreover the word of the Lord came to me, saying, "Jeremiah, what do you see?" And I said, "I see a branch of an almond tree." Then the Lord said to me, "You have seen well, for I am ready to perform My word." And the word of the Lord came to me the second time, saying, "What do you see?" And I said, "I see a boiling pot, and it is facing away from the north."*

In this Scripture, we see where God tested the prophetic understanding and growth of His prophets, to see whether or not they understood the times and seasons.

Generally speaking, the almond tree blooms early in the spring. It is the first tree to bloom in the winter; and when it blossoms, it is symbolic of spring in the air. In the Hebrew culture, the almond tree and the action of Jeremiah watching (as a watchman would) symbolizes new season, hope, joy and resurrection. It meant things would begin to spring forth again. To some extent it meant replenishing and restoration. The prophet of God must know what season they are in so that they could accurately guide the nation. It also represents God swiftly fulfilling His promise of upcoming exile and destruction. The almond tree blossoms as early in the season. This showed imminent calamity for the wicked.

# Bitter And Sweet

Almond comes in 2 species – bitter and sweet. So, we will see the manifestation of 2 events – bitter and sweet. Ultimately, we will see redemption and destruction.

Jeremiah 31: 27 – 28 reminds us, "Behold, the days are coming, says the Lord, that I will sow the house of Israel and the house of Judah with the seed of man and the seed of beast. And it shall come to pass, that as I have watched over them to pluck up, to break down, to throw down, to destroy, and to afflict, so I will watch over them to build and to plant, says the Lord."

While God's faithful will walk in prosperity, the enemies of God will experience the judgement of God.

While God watches over His people, He will build up and plant them. However, the enemy will be uprooted and broken down. Breakdown is a must in order to build. We will see this happen globally.

The Hebrew meaning for the word *"almond"* is *"sha-kade"* and the root of the word *"almond,"* *"sha-ked,"* is identical to the verb *"sha-kad,"* which means *"to be diligent, to strive, steadfast."* These are the qualities that any good watchman must possess.

God has a time to perform every prophetic word – whether positive or negative. We are in a time where God is ready to perform His word, hence, the watchman must watch, hasten, anticipate, be sleepless, alert, vigilant and on the look-out.

## Spring Begins

In the Northern Hemisphere this year, Spring begins on March 20, 2022 and ends on June 21, 2022. So, in the first 19 days of March, we need to be on the watch. It is important to note that while Spring happens in the Northern Hemisphere – in countries such as Canada, the USA, the Caribbean Islands and the West Indies, it is Winter in the Southern Hemisphere – in countries such as Australia, New Zealand, Antarctica, major parts of South America, about one-third of Africa, and some islands of mainland Asia.

Jeremiah 1: 13 – 15 speaks of the calamity and terror that will come out of the North. The Babylonians are the major instruments used by God to punish His enemies. Interestingly, the Northernmost nations of the world include Greenland/Denmark, Canada, Russia, Norway, United States, Finland, Sweden, and Iceland. Today, most if not all of these nations are hotbeds of activity.

## The Boiling Pot

The Boiling Pot represents God's judgement, calamity and terror, from the north, since during that time most of the invaders of Israel and Judah came from that direction.

The steam of this boiling pot represented God's judgments, which are often compared to a fire, as the afflictions of

Israel were to a smoking furnace. (Jeremiah 1: 13; Genesis 15:17.)

The Boiling Pot also symbolizes doctrine, traditions, determination through a person. The pot further denoted the empire of the Chaldeans, lying to the north of Judea, and pouring forth its multitudes like a thick vapor.

Are the nations ready to deal with the judgement calamity and terror that is about to come upon the globe? It is critical therefore, for the peoples of the nations to stock up on the following:

| | | |
|---|---|---|
| Masks | Sanitizers | Toothpaste |
| Bleach | Wipes | Pampers |
| Pull-ups | Baby Formula | Bath Soap |
| Lamps | Candles | Matches |
| Olive Oil | Garlic | Tents |
| Basins / Tubs | Water | Vitamins |
| Medical Supplies | Batteries | Canned Goods |
| Feminine Products | Matches/Lighters | |

# BIBLIOGRAPHY

Hayford, Jack W. Executive Editor, New Spirit-Filled Life ® Bible, (New King James Version © 2002 Thomas Nelson, Inc.

www.rwominc.com
www.lystonvoice.com

www.ingramcontent.com/pod-product-compliance
Lightning Source LLC
Chambersburg PA
CBHW061631040426
42446CB00010B/1364